THE COMING MAN

Edited by Philip P. Choy, Lorraine Dong, and Marlon K. Hom

COMING MAN

19th Century American Perceptions of the Chinese

University of Washington Press
Seattle and London

CONTENTS

LIST OF PLATES

1   The Coming Man—Scene on the Pier of the Pacific Mail Steamship Company, San Francisco—Passengers Disembarking and Being Received by Their Friends (artist unknown)
    [*Frank Leslie's Illustrated Newspaper*, 7 May 1870]

2   Chinese Emigration to America—Sketch on Board the Pacific Mail Steamship "Alaska" (artist unknown)
    [*Harper's Weekly*, 20 May 1876, pp. 408-409]

3   Sunday Service on Board a Pacific Mail Steamship (artist: Felix Regamy)
    [*Harper's Weekly*, 16 June 1877, p. 461]

4   Arrival of a Shipload of Chinese Women at San Francisco—The Celestial Ladies Riding from the Dock in Express Wagons (artist unknown)
    [*Frank Leslie's Illustrated Newspaper*, 10 April 1869, p. 56]

5   Chinese Quarters, Virginia City, Nevada (artist: W.A. Rogers)
    [*Harper's Weekly*, 29, Dec. 1877, p. 1025]

6   Chinesen-Quartier in Sacramento, California (artist unknown)
    [*Frank Leslie's Illustrierte Zeitung*, 9 Aug. 1878, p. 153]

7   A Street in Chinatown, San Francisco (from a picture by Miss G.A. Davis)
    [*Frank Leslie's Illustrated Newspaper*, 15 Aug. 1891]

8   Sunday Afternoon in Chinatown, Los Angeles, California—Singing Hymns in the Street (artist: Charles Mente)
    [*Harper's Weekly*, 18 Aug. 1894]

9   The Coming Man—An Evening Scene in the Chinese Quarter, San Francisco, Cal.—The Chinese Vegetable and Meat Peddlers on Their Rounds (artist unknown)
    [*Frank Leslie's Illustrated Newspaper*, 23 July 1870, p. 301]

10   A Street Scene in the Chinese Quarter of San Francisco, Cal., During the Celebration of the Chinese New Year's (artist: Joseph Becker)
      [*Frank Leslie's Illustrated Newspaper*, 6 March 1875, p. 425]

11   The Chinese Colony at Belleville, N.J.—Celebration of the Celestial New Year, February 14th (artist unknown)
      [*Harper's Weekly*, 9 March 1877]

12   A Wedding in the Chinese Quarter—Mott Street, New York (artist: W.A. Rogers)
      [*Harper's Weekly*, 22, Nov. 1890, pp. 908-909]

13   New York's Strange Theatres. Typical Views of the Hebrew and Chinese Play-Houses, Which Visitors to the City Find Particularly Interesting (artist: Hy Mayer)
      [*Leslie's Weekly*, 18 Nov. 1899, p. 400]

14   Chinesen-Quartier in San Francisco, California (artist unknown)
      [*Frank Leslie's Illustrierte Zeitung*, 9 Aug. 1878, p. 152]

15   A Chinese Burial in Lone Mountain Cemetery, San Francisco, California (artist: Paul Frenzeny)
      [*Harper's Weekly*, 28 Jan. 1882, p. 56]

16   The Coming Man—Scene in the Hallway of a House in the Chinese Quarter, San Francisco—A Chinese Girl Making an Offering in Memory of the Dead & Scene in a Joss-House in the Chinese Quarter, San Francisco—A Chinese Merchant Burning Prayers That His Ventures May Prove Fortunate (artist unknown)
      [*Frank Leslie's Illustrated Newspaper*, 18 June 1870, p. 221]

17   California—Chinese Mission-School at the Methodist Chapel, Jackson Street, San Francisco (artist: Hyde)
      [*Frank Leslie's Illustrated Newspaper*, 15 April 1876, p. 97]

18   The Chinese School in Mott Street, New York (artist: W.P. Snyder)
      [*Harper's Weekly*, 19 July 1879, p. 573]

19   The Chinese College at Hartford, Connecticut (from sketches by Theo. R. Davis)
      [*Harper's Weekly*, 18 May 1878, p. 396]

20   Among the Chinese on the Pacific Coast (artist: T. Langguth)
      [*Harper's Weekly*, 22 Oct. 1880, p. 508]

21   The Coming Man—Scene in the Chinese Quarter, San Francisco—Interior View of a Chinese

Silversmith's Shop (artist unknown)
[*Frank Leslie's Illustrated Newspaper*, 14 May 1870, p. 141]

22   Weighing Out Medicines in a Chinese Drug-Store, San Francisco (artist: W.A. Rogers)
[*Harper's Weekly*, 9 Dec. 1899, p. 1239]

23   Chinese Merchants Exchange, San Francisco (artist: P. Frenzeny)
[*Harper's Weekly*, 18 March 1882, p. 173]

24   San Francisco, Cal.—A Chinese Rag-Picker (artist unknown)
[source unknown]

25   A Chinaman en Route for the Mines (artist unknown)
[*Gleason's Pictorial Drawing Room Companion*, ca. 1852, p. 277]

26   Chinese Camp in the Mines (artist: J.D. Borthwick)
[J.D. Borthwick, *3 Years in California* (1857), n.p.]

27   Chinese Fishermen in San Francisco Bay (artists: Frenzeny and Tavernier)
[*Harper's Weekly*, 20 March 1875, p. 240]

28   Across the Continent. The Snow Sheds on the Central Pacific Railroad, in the Sierra Nevada Mountains
(from a sketch by Joseph Becker)
[source unknown; ca. 1869]

29   "Chinese Cheap Labor" in Louisiana,—Chinamen at Work on the Milloudon Sugar Plantation (artist
unknown)
[*Every Saturday*, 29 July 1871, p. 113]

30   Grape and Hop Culture in California. (1) A Grape-Picker. (2) San Rafael, with Mount Tamalpais in the
Distance. (3) Hop Ranch and Vineyards, St. Helena (artist: Charles Graham)
[*Harper's Weekly*, 21 Jan. 1888, p. 44]

31   The Vintage in California—At Work at the Wine-Presses (artist: P. Frenzeny)
[*Harper's Weekly*, 5 Oct. 1878, pp. 792-3]

32   The Wine-Vault in a Southern California Vineyard (artist: W.A. Rogers)
[*Harper's Weekly*, ca. 1879, p. 1126]

33   California—Phases of Chinese Labor in San Francisco: (1) Chinese Laundry-Work in the Palace
Hotel—The Steam Mangle. (2) Chinese Laundry Work in the Palace Hotel—The Steam Centrifugal

Wringer. (3) Shaving, Cleansing and Scraping Heads in a Basement Barber-Shop. (artist: H.A. Ogden)
[*Frank Leslie's Illustrated Newspaper*, 7 June 1879, p. 228]

34 The Coming Man—A Chinese Laundry in San Francisco, California—The Coming Man Washing, Drying, Sprinkling, and Ironing Clothes (artist unknown)
[*Frank Leslie's Illustrated Newspaper*, 14 May 1870, p. 141]

35 The Coming Man—A Chinese Cigar Manufacturing in San Francisco—Preparing the Tobacco-Leaf and Making Cigars (artist unknown)
[*Frank Leslie's Illustrated Newspaper*, 21 May 1870, p. 152]

36 The Avant-Couriers of the Coming Man—Chinamen in the Bottomers' Room in Sampson's Factory, at North Adams, Massachusetts, Being Instructed in the Art of Making Shoes (artist unknown)
[*Frank Leslie's Illustrated Newspaper*, 9 July 1870, p. 264]

37 The Avant-Couriers of the Coming Man—Scene in Sampson's Shoe Manufactory, at North Adams, Massachusetts—Teaching the Chinese the Use of the Pegging Machine (artist unknown)
[*Frank Leslie's Illustrated Newspaper*, 9 July 1870, p. 264]

38 "The Open Door!" (artist: W.A. Rogers)
[*Harper's Weekly*, 5 Aug. 1899]

39 A Fair Field and No Favor! (artist: W.A. Rogers)
[*Harper's Weekly*, 18 Nov. 1899]

40 The First Duty (artist unknown)
[*Puck*, 8 Aug. 1900]

41 Reception of the Hon. Anson Burlingame and Members of the Chinese Embassy, by the Traveler's Club, May 30th 1868, at the Club House, 222 Fifth Avenue, New York City (artist unknown)
[*Frank Leslie's Illustrated Newspaper*, 20 June 1868, p. 216]

42 California—Arrival at San Francisco of the First Resident Embassy of the Chinese Empire Accredited to the United States—Officers of the "Six Companies" Welcoming Chin Lan Pin and the Consular Corps in the Cabin of the "City of Tokio," July 25th (artist unknown)
[*Frank Leslie's Illustrated Newspaper*, 17 Aug. 1878]

43 California—Arrival at San Francisco of the First Resident Embassy of the Chinese Empire Accredited to the United States, July 25th: (1) Chinese Merchants of San Francisco Paying Their Respects to the Embassy in the Grand Parlor of the Palace Hotel. (2) Arrival of the Embassy, Escorted by Resident Merchants at the Reception Saloon of the Hotel. (3) Members of the Embassy Promenading in the Lobby

of the Hotel After Dining (artist unknown)
[*Frank Leslie's Illustrated Newspaper*, 17 Aug. 1878, pp. 494-495]

44   The Chasm of Defeat Awaits His Uncertain Tread (artist: Walter)
[*The Wasp*, 27 Oct. 1880, pp. 8-9]

45   "The Chinese Must Come." Grover and Gresham Dallying with Their Pets Once More (artist: T.L.)
[*The Wasp*, ca. 1894, pp. 10-11]

46   How They Will Evade the Chinese Treaty (artist: Walter)
[*The Wasp*, 31 May 1888, pp. 8-9]

47   Where Both Platforms Agree—No Vote—No Use to Either Party (artist: J.A. Wales)
[*Puck*, 14 July 1880]

48   The Anti-Chinese Wall. The American Wall Goes Up as the Chinese Original Goes Down (artist: F. Gratz)
[*Puck*, 29 March 1882, pp. 56-57]

49   The Right Man in the Right Place (artist: C.J. Taylor)
[*Puck*, 11 March 1891]

50   As the Heathen See Us—A Meeting of the Chinese Missions Society (artist: J.S. Pughe)
[source unknown; lithograph by J. Ottmann Lith. Co., Puck Bldg., New York, c. 1900]

51   The Ultimate Cause (artist: Frank A. Namkivel)
[*Puck*, 12 Dec. 1900]

52   "On Earth Peace, Good-Will Toward Men" (artist: Thomas Nast)
[*Harper's Weekly*, 27 Dec. 1884]

53   Arbitration Is the True Balance of Power (artist: J. Keppler)
[*Puck*, 17 March 1886, pp. 40-41]

54   What Shall We Do with Our Boys? (artist: Keller)
[*The Wasp*, ca. 1870s, pp. 136-7]

55   The Chinese: Many Handed But Soulless (artist: S)
[*The Wasp*, 14 Nov. 1885]

56   The Coming Man (artist: Keller)

[*The Wasp*, 20 May 1881, p. 336]

57   Boot and Shoemakers' White Labor League (1891 Broadsheet)

58   Swords of Damocles (artist: Keller)
      [*The Wasp*, March 1882, pp. 656-7]

59   The Modern St. George (artist: Keller)
      [*The Wasp*, 9 April 1881, p. 240)

60   When Will This Ass Kick (artist: Keller)
      [*The Wasp*, 20 May 1881, pp. 328-9]

61   The First Blow at the Chinese Question (artist: Keller)
      [*The Wasp*, 8 Dec. 1877]

62   A Trio That Must Go (artist: F. Graetz)
      [*Puck*, 5 Sep. 1883]

63   Political Capital and Compound Interest (artist: Thomas Nast)
      [*Harper's Weekly*, 31 Jan. 1880, p. 68]

64   The Ides of March (artist: Thomas Nast)
      [*Harper's Weekly*, 20 Mar. 1880]

65   California—The Chinese Agitation in San Francisco—A Meeting of the Workingmen's Party on the
      Sand Lots (from a sketch by H.A. Rodgers)
      [*Frank Leslie's Illustrated Newspaper*, 20 March 1880, p. 41]

66   The New Comet—A Phenomenon Now Visible in All Parts of the United States (artist: Thomas Nast)
      [*Harper's Weekly*, 6 Aug. 1870, p. 505]

67   The Pigtail Has Got to Go (artist: Wolnymple)
      [*Puck*, 19 Oct. 1898]

68   The Bubonic Plague in San Francisco. Chinamen, Confined Within the Chinese Quarter, Cooking Their
      Meals (artist unknown)
      [*Harper's Weekly*, 2 June 1900, p. 505]

69   A Haunt of the Highbinders in Chinatown. The Chinese Highbinders in San Francisco (artist unknown)
      [*Harper's Weekly*, 13 Feb. 1886, p. 100]

83   Uncle Sam's Thanksgiving Dinner (artist: Thomas Nast)
      [*Harper's Weekly*, 20 Nov. 1869, p. 745]

84   What Shall We Do with John Chinaman? (artist unknown)
      [*Frank Leslie's Illustrated Newspaper*, 25 Sep. 1869, p. 32]

85   Pennsylvania—War of Races in the City of Brotherly Love—Colored Washerwomen Berating Chinese
      Laundrymen (artist: Regamey)
      [*Frank Leslie's Illustrated Newspaper*, 29 May 1875, p. 189]

86   The Chinese Invasion (artist: Keppler)
      [*Puck*, n.d., pp. 24-25]

87   Consequences of Coolieism (artist: Walter)
      [*The Wasp*, 7 Nov. 1885, p. 16]

88   In the Clutches of the Chinese Tiger (artist: unknown)
      [*The Wasp*, 7 Nov. 1885, p. 8]

89   The Ship of State Glided Noiselessly to Her Doom (artist: G.F. Keller)
      [P.W. Dooner, *Last Days of the Republic* (San Francisco: Alta California Publishing House, 1880), n.p.]

90   The Beginning of the End (artist: G.F. Keller)
      [P.W. Dooner, *Last Days of the Republic* (San Francisco: Alta California Publishing House, 1880), n.p.]

91   The War of the Races (artist: G.F. Keller)
      [P.W. Dooner, *Last Days of the Republic* (San Francisco: Alta California Publishing House, 1880), n.p.]

92   The Mandarins in Washington (artist: G.F. Keller)
      [P.W. Dooner, *Last Days of the Republic* (San Francisco: Alta California Publishing House, 1880), n.p.]

93   The Governor of California (artist: G.F. Keller)
      [P.W. Dooner, *Last Days of the Republic* (San Francisco: Alta California Publishing House, 1880), n.p.]

94   The "Fourth" of the Future (artist: J.B. Arkhaus)
      [*The Wasp*, n.d., pp. 8-9]

95   Pacific Railroad Complete (artist: W.L. Palin)
      [*Harper's Weekly*, 12 June 1869, p. 384]

96   The Last Addition to the Family (artist: Hunk E. Dore)

[*Harper's Weekly*, n.d., p. 624]

97   A Statue for Our Harbor (artist: Keller)
     [*The Wasp*, 11 Nov. 1881, p. 320]

98   "The Mountain in Labor" (Aesop's Fables) (artist: Keller)
     [*The Wasp*, 1882, p. 158]

99   Will It Come to This? (artist unknown)
     [*The Wasp*, ca. 1870s, pp. 152-3]

100 San Francisco. Must I Support Them All? (artist unknown)
     [*The Wasp*, 27 Feb. 1886, p. 16]

101 Colorado—The Anti Chinese Riot in Denver, on October 31st (artist: N.B. Wilkins)
     [*Frank Leslie's Illustrated Newspaper*, 20 Nov. 1880, p. 189)

102 The Massacre of the Chinese at Rock Springs, Wyoming (artist: T. de Thul from photographs by C.A. Booth)
     [*Harper's Weekly*, 26 Sep. 1885, p. 637]

103 The Chinese Commission at Rock Springs (from photographs by C.A. Booth)
     [*Harper's Weekly*, 17 Oct. 1885, p. 676]

104 Untitled (artist: J.A. Wales)
     [*Puck*, 17 March 1886]

105 The Anti-Chinese Riot at Seattle, Washington Territory. (1) Driving Chinamen on Board of the Steamer. (2) Marching Under Guard to the Court-house (artist: W.P. Snyder)
     [*Harper's Weekly*, 6 March 1886, p. 157]

106 Hard Pushing (artist: Keller)
     [*The Wasp*, 7 May 1881]

107 His Hands Tied (artist: F.A.)
     [*The Wasp*, 14 April 1882]

108 Amusing the Child (artist: Keller)
     [*The Wasp*, 19 May 1882, p. 320)

109 Law Rules Here—Diplomacy at Washington (artist unknown)

INTRODUCTION

Historical Background

The coming of the Chinese to America about one hundred and forty years ago is part of a complex economic relationship between China and America. This influx became the focal point for America's ensuing foreign and domestic policies that often conflicted with each other, with the United States usually holding the upper hand.

Since its birth as a nation in 1776, the United States has sought to establish commercial relations with China. After the annexation of territories west of the Mississippi to the Pacific Coast, particularly after incorporating California in 1848, the United States reached across the Pacific to China, wanting to acquire and hold equal positions of power and influence alongside stronger European powers. In 1844, after the conclusion of the Opium War, the United States and China signed a treaty, known as the Wang-Hea [Wangxia; aka Wang-Hia] Treaty, to establish "peace, amity, and commerce" between the two nations. Its purpose was to establish and extend America's economic interests in China.

The 1848 discovery of gold in California attracted thousands of Chinese, mostly Cantonese, to mainland United States. Subsequently the Chinese were also recruited as a major source of labor in the economic development of the American West. Thousands of Chinese were recruited for the construction of the Transcontinental Railroad during the early 1860s. In the state of California, the Chinese comprised the bulk of farm laborers and helped reclaim swamps into farmlands. By the 1870s, the Chinese were also active in urban industry, manufacturing shirts, shoes, boots, and cigars. In 1880, the Chinese population in the continental United States reached 105,000, about .002% of the total population. However, in the state of California alone, the Chinese made up 10% of the population. White workers, faced with a widespread economic depression at national, state, and local levels, saw the growing number of Chinese laborers as responsible for white unemployment.

Special interest groups that lobbied for Chinese exclusion led to anti-Chinese hysteria. Under pressure from the United States, a weak Chinese Manchu government signed the 1880 Angell Treaty in which China voluntarily restricted its own citizens from going to America. The treaty opened the doors for Congress to pass an exclusion bill barring the entry of all Chinese laborers. President Chester A. Arthur eventually signed the Chinese Exclusion Act on May 6, 1882.

The passage of the 1882 Act and its subsequent amendments

and related acts in 1884, 1888, 1892, 1893, 1898, 1901, 1902, and 1904, banned the entry of both skilled and unskilled Chinese laborers, which climaxed with the 1924 Immigration Act that extended exclusion to all Asians. The Chinese Exclusion Acts dramatically altered the coming of the Chinese to America. They exempted Chinese

merchants, visitors, teachers, students, and diplomats, but in practice effectively denied entry to all Chinese who intended to immigrate. In addition, provisions in the acts extended the exclusion to certain classes of Chinese women and disallowed the Chinese from becoming naturalized United States citizens. By 1920, the Chinese American population in the continental United States, including the American-born generation, was reduced to less than 62,000, slightly more than one-half of the 1880 total.

The 1882 Chinese Exclusion Act was the first federal law to bar immigration on the basis of race and class. Championed by white American labor, Chinese exclusion became known as the "Chinese Question" in domestic politics. It occupied the nation's politics from the 1870s to 1900s. Racism, particularly in the form of xenophobia, further intensified the labor versus capital conflict. This 19th century Sinophobia, later known as the "Yellow Peril," took

root as the Chinese became scapegoats of the American labor movement in the West. Writings on the "Chinese Question" pro and con abound in federal and state legislation and the press. Most debates degenerated into racial harangues, stressing "white" superiority over "yellow" inferiority.

The Chinese Exclusion Act and its subsequent amendments were finally repealed in 1943, brought about by the alliance between China and the United States against Japanese military aggression in Asia. Economic and political factors as well played crucial roles in the alliance. On December 17, 1943, as a gesture of goodwill, President Franklin D. Roosevelt signed the Repeal Act, ending sixty-one years of exclusion.

Political Cartoons

Political and editorial cartoons are drawings that comment on an event/situation or a public/political personage. This form of art expression can be either humorous, vindictive, or satirical, but almost always condescending. It is believed that the first political cartoon to appear in an American newspaper was on the May 9, 1754 issue of Benjamin Franklin's *Pennsylvania Gazette*. The 19th century saw issues emerging that were ripe for this particular medium. By the 1890s, pictorial illustrations and political cartoons could be found in almost every daily newspaper.

The title of this book, "The Coming Man," is borrowed from the series of pictorials published by *Leslie's Illustrated Newspaper* in 1870, and is not to be confused with *The Wasp*'s "Coming Man" (Plate 56). The drawings exemplify how America recognized the Chinese presence and the predictions of what would follow. They began mainly as an expression of cultural curiosity, so the Chinese were seen as benign and non-competitive, and their physiognomy was drawn accordingly without malicious caricature. Because America was in its infantile stage of understanding China, cultural inaccuracies com-

pounded by artistic license and flaw were inevitable. Chinese written characters would be "drawn" nonsensically and the women's hairdos were exaggerated. Such illustrations would later degenerate into vicious political cartoons as America's China foreign policy and its domestic politics came into conflict.

When anti-Chinese sentiment intensified and the need arose to justify federal passage of a Chinese exclusion law, the Chinese became the inevitable target of political cartoonists. Sino-American relationship and American versus Chinese politics dominated political headlines for thirty years, becoming favorite issues for political satire. Newspapers and magazines, with corresponding articles or editorials, maximized the art form to portray Chinese stereotypically as caricatures representing "ugly" and "irrepressible" heathens.

The following compilation, selected from the private collection of Mr. Philip P. Choy and augmented from the archives of the

Chinese Historical Society of America, provides samples of early pictorials and political cartoons published in popular literature in the latter half of the 19th century. There are a total of 116 illustrations (13 from the Society archives), plus one broadsheet, dating from 1869 to 1900. Forty-four of them were originally published in color.

The majority of the pictorials were printed in widely circulated national publications such as *Harper's Weekly* and *Leslie's Illustrated Newspaper*, or regional magazines like *The Wasp* (San Francisco) and *Puck* (New York). Some were drawn by famous artists like G. Frederick Keller, J.

Langstruth, and Thomas Nast, the latter of whom created the elephant and donkey symbols for the Republican and Democrat parties respectively. Although the circulation of these publications ran from 80,000 to 400,000 during their peak, the readership of these newspapers were most likely urban, literate white men. Few were read by Chinese or other minorities. Hence, the intent and impact of these cartoons must be viewed from the perspective of a white male readership. The selection offers the reader an opportunity to turn back the pages of history and experience the hostility and tension during the Chinese exclusion era. It also reveals the racist atmosphere of the 19th century, a legacy we have yet to resolve in 20th century America.

Community Life

I. COMMUNITY LIFE

When the Chinese first arrived in the United States, they were considered a curiosity. Chinese settlements known as Chinatown, Little China, or Little Canton became a novelty. Many early tabloids began to depict the Chinese without derision, but rather for their attraction as newsworthy subjects.

Leslie's Illustrated Newspaper began "The Coming Man" series in 1870 to inform the public of the presence of the Chinese people on the Pacific coast. Every illustration was accompanied with extensive textual explanations, some of which were pedantic in nature and oftentimes culturally patronizing. The following is an excerpt from the first issue of "The Coming Man":

The Chinese are tractable, industrious and thrifty; and, although they may never aspire to office, or influence "political rings," will, if not persecuted beyond human endurance, make intelligent, lawabiding citizens. Give them an opportunity "to work out their salvation." If this is granted, we are quite sure they will soon slough off all that is hurtful that comes to them from their old civilization and readily adapt themselves to the newer and higher life which finds its birth in this century of our era.
(*Frank Leslie's Illustrated Newspaper*, 7 May 1870, p. 114)

This section begins with pictures depicting the Chinese arrival (Plates 1-4), followed by drawings revealing the diversity of the Chinese people in America during the 1800s: their daily activities, and where and how they lived (Plates 5-24). Plates 25-37 not only illustrate the Chinese being recruited to work in the New England states (Plates 36 and 37) and the South (Plate 29), but more importantly, that they were a major force in the economic development of the American West.

1   The Coming Man—Scene on the Pier of the Pacific Mail Steamship
         Company, San Francisco—Passengers Disembarking and Being Received
         by Their Friends

2   Chinese Emigration to America—Sketch on Board the Pacific Mail Steamship "Alaska"

3   Sunday Service on Board a Pacific Mail Steamship

The Coming Man

4   Arrival of a Shipload of Chinese Women at San Francisco—The Celestial Ladies Riding from the Dock in Express Wagons

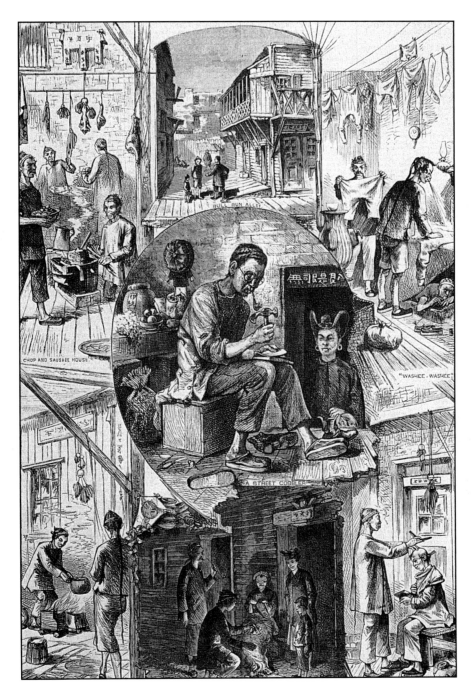

5   Chinese Quarters, Virginia City, Nevada

6   Chinesen-Quartier in Sacramento, California

7   A Street in Chinatown, San Francisco

8   Sunday Afternoon in Chinatown, Los Angeles, California—Singing Hymns
        in the Street

9   The Coming Man—An Evening Scene in the Chinese Quarter, San
        Francisco, Cal.—The Chinese Vegetable and Meat Peddlers on Their
        Rounds

10   A Street Scene in the Chinese Quarter of San Francisco, Cal., During the Celebration of the Chinese New Year's

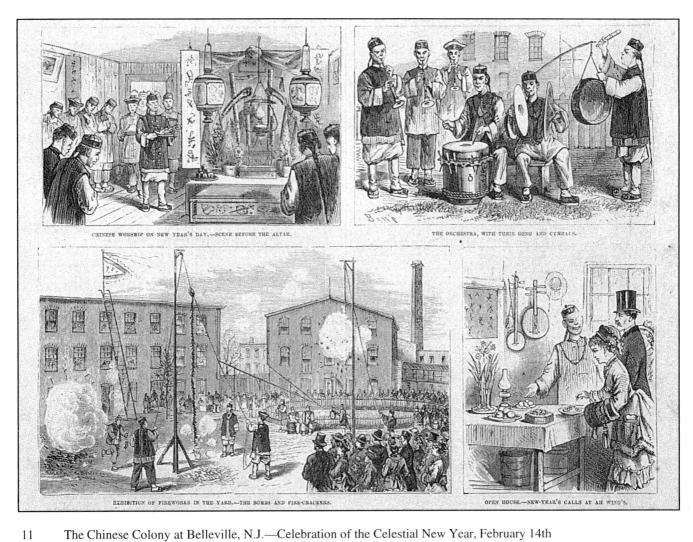

CHINESE WORSHIP ON NEW YEAR'S DAY.—SCENE BEFORE THE ALTAR.

THE ORCHESTRA, WITH THEIR GONG AND CYMBALS.

EXHIBITION OF FIREWORKS IN THE YARD.—THE BOMBS AND FIRE-CRACKERS.

OPEN HOUSE.—NEW-YEAR'S CALLS AT AH WING'S.

11   The Chinese Colony at Belleville, N.J.—Celebration of the Celestial New Year, February 14th

12   A Wedding in the Chinese Quarter—Mott Street, New York

13   New York's Strange Theatres. Typical Views of the Hebrew and Chinese Play-Houses, Which Visitors to the City Find Particularly Interesting

14   Chinesen-Quartier in San Francisco, California

15   A Chinese Burial in Lone Mountain Cemetery, San Francisco, California

16   The Coming Man—Scene in the Hallway of a House in the Chinese Quarter, San Francisco—A Chinese
        Girl Making an Offering in Memory of the Dead & Scene in a Joss-House in the Chinese Quarter, San
        Francisco—A Chinese Merchant Burning Prayers That His Ventures May Prove Fortunate

17   California—Chinese Mission-School at the Methodist Chapel, Jackson Street, San Francisco

18   The Chinese School in Mott Street, New York

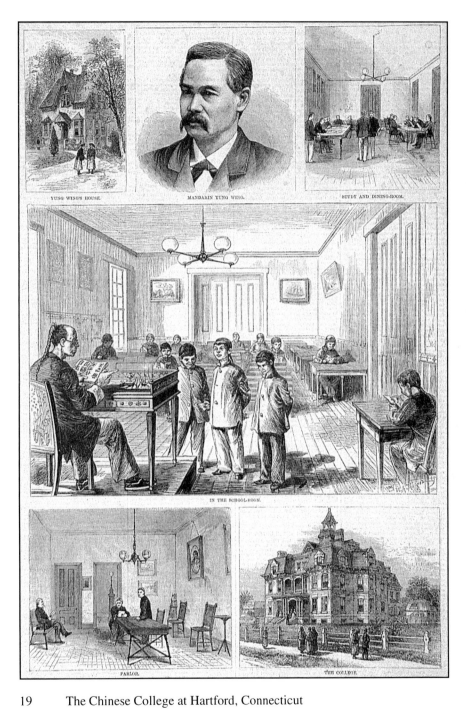

19   The Chinese College at Hartford, Connecticut

20   Among the Chinese on the Pacific Coast

21   The Coming Man—Scene in the Chinese Quarter, San Francisco—Interior View of a Chinese Silversmith's Shop

The Coming Man

22   Weighing Out Medicines in a Chinese Drug-Store, San Francisco

23   Chinese Merchants Exchange, San Francisco

26   Chinese Camp in the Mines

27   Chinese Fishermen in San Francisco Bay

28   Across the Continent. The Snow Sheds on the Central Pacific Railroad, in the Sierra Nevada Mountains

29   "Chinese Cheap Labor" in Louisiana,—Chinamen at Work on the Milloudon Sugar Plantation

30   Grape and Hop Culture in California. (1) A Grape-Picker. (2) San Rafael, with
        Mount Tamalpais in the Distance. (3) Hop Ranch and Vineyards, St. Helena

31   The Vintage in California—At Work at the Wine-Presses

32   The Wine-Vault in a Southern California Vineyard

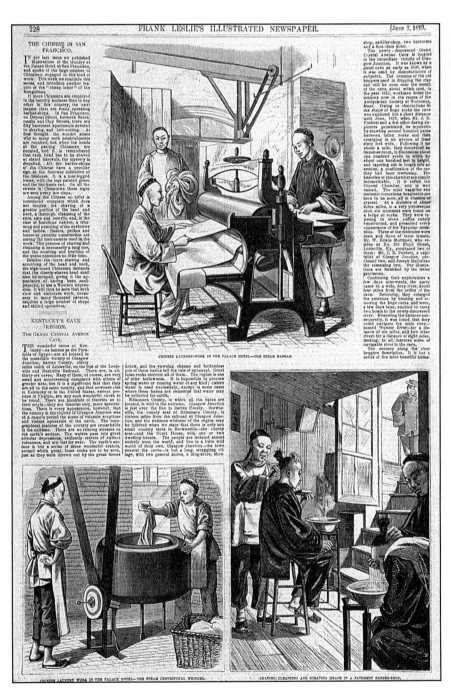

228   FRANK LESLIE'S ILLUSTRATED NEWSPAPER.   [JUNE 7, 1879.

CHINESE LAUNDRY-WORK IN THE PALACE HOTEL—THE STEAM MANGLE.

CHINESE LAUNDRY WORK IN THE PALACE HOTEL—THE STEAM CENTRIFUGAL WRINGER.

SHAVING, CLEANSING AND SCRAPING HEADS IN A BASEMENT BARBER-SHOP.

33   California—Phases of Chinese Labor in San Francisco: (1) Chinese Laundry-Work in the Palace Hotel—The Steam Mangle. (2) Chinese Laundry Work in the Palace Hotel—The Steam Centrifugal Wringer. (3) Shaving, Cleansing and Scraping Heads in a Basement Barber-Shop.

33

34   The Coming Man—A Chinese Laundry in San Francisco, California—The Coming Man Washing, Drying, Sprinkling, and Ironing Clothes

35   The Coming Man—A Chinese Cigar Manufacturing in San Francisco—Preparing the Tobacco-Leaf and Making Cigars

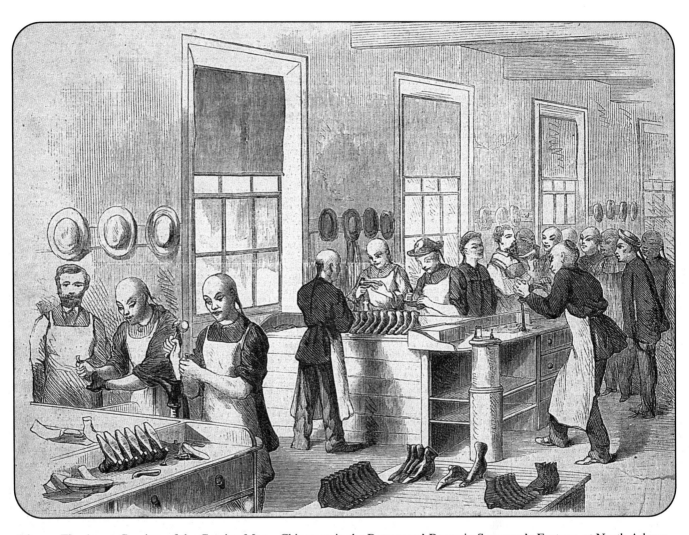

36   The Avant-Couriers of the Coming Man—Chinamen in the Bottomers' Room in Sampson's Factory, at North Adams,
        Massachusetts, Being Instructed in the Art of Making Shoes

37   The Avant-Couriers of the Coming Man—Scene in Sampson's Shoe Manufactory, at North Adams, Massachusetts—Teaching the Chinese the Use of the Pegging Machine

II

Sino-American Relations

II. SINO-AMERICAN RELATIONS

Like the European countries that entered into treaty agreements unfavorable to China, the United States likewise wanted the same advantages for any potential economic and political gain in China (Plates 48-50):

Our Treaty rights in the Celestial Empire...are all perfectly clear. Under the "most favored nation" clause we enjoy all the commercial privileges granted by China to any of our competitors.
(*Harper's Weekly*, 18 Nov. 1899, p. 1154)

The Wang-Hea Treaty of Peace, Amity, and Commerce was signed on July 3, 1844, between the United States and China in order to establish a "firm, lasting, and sin- cere friendship between the two nations...by means of a treaty or general convention of peace, am- ity, and commerce." In 1858, the treaty was renewed as the Sino- American Treaty of Tientsin [Tianjin].

The United States interest in an "open China" was dictated by ambitious traders with visions of commercial prosperity and mission- aries with religious zeal to spread the Christian gospel. At that time, the United States was thinking only about reaching into China; the com- ing of Chinese settlers to the United States was never anticipated. American immigration had been primarily white European, with black Africans arriving mainly un- der the European-controlled slave trade.

On July 28, 1868, further additions to the Tientsin Treaty were made and ratified as the 1868 Supplementary Articles to the Sino- American Treaty of Tientsin. This is better known as the Burlingame Treaty. The 1868 treaty was the work of three Americans: Anson Burlingame, a former American minister to China who became En- voy Extraordinary and Minister Plenipotentiary of the Emperor of China to Foreign Powers; U.S. Sec- retary of State William Seward; and S. Wells Williams, a mission- ary, translator, and close friend of Burlingame (Plate 41). Some key provisions under the Burlingame Treaty were the abrogation of the Chinese government's prohibition on emigration and the appointment of Chinese consuls to American ports. This was meant to facilitate trading and emigration between the two countries, which resulted in a large-scale entry of Chinese laborers to America. It was not intended for the Chinese to settle and become a part of the American society. Article VI stated specifi- cally that "nothing herein contained shall be held to confer naturalization...upon the subjects of China in the United States."

Meanwhile, the Chinese in America under the leadership of the Chinese Six Companies wanted the Chinese government to establish diplomatic missions to look after their interests in the United States. Nine years later in 1878, the Chinese government finally appointed Chen Lanbin as its first minister plenipotentiary to the United States (Plates 42-43). Yung Wing [Rong Hong], who already had a position with the Chinese Educational Mission at Hartford, Connecticut (Plate 19), served as associate minister plenipotentiary. This was to set the stage for cordial and friendly diplomatic relations.

With the ratification of the Burlingame Treaty, the Chinese began to enter the labor market. Nativism swelled in the minds of Americans. Anti-Chinese sentiment and movements emerged and intensified in the 1870s, and the Chinese were viewed as an economic threat. America's foreign policies and relations with China were forced to yield to the domestic policies at home. In an effort to get rid of all Chinese labor, it was necessary to revise the Burlingame Treaty. President Rutherford S. Hayes appointed James B. Angell,

president of the University of Michigan, as minister plenipotentiary to China and chief delegate of the commission for revising treaties with China. A new treaty was negotiated and signed in 1880, wherein the "Government of China agrees that the Government of the United States may regulate, limit, or suspend such coming or residence [of Chinese laborers], but may not absolutely prohibit it." All Chinese residing in America would be protected by the United States government.

The 1880 Angell Treaty provided the pretext needed by anti-Chinese lobbyists to push for Chinese exclusion in the United States. Meanwhile, European laborers were encouraged to come as "cheap" labor (Plate 44). The Chinese government vehemently protested the various ensuing exclusion acts passed by Congress. In an attempt to resolve any treaty violations, Chinese envoy Yang Ru and Secretary of State Walter Q. Gresham were assigned to modify the 1880 treaty. Using the term

"necessary regulation," the resulting 1894 Gresham-Yang Treaty completely prohibited Chinese laborers from entering the United States for ten years and placed China on the defensive by stating that the Chinese government, "in view of the antagonism and much deprecated and serious disorders to which the presence of Chinese laborers has given rise in certain parts of the United States, desires to prohibit the emigration of such laborers from China to the United States." The treaty also voided the 1888 Scott Act which barred the re-entry of about 20,000 Chinese laborers who held valid re-entry permits to the United States. This plus the Act of September 13, 1888 stipulation that allowed Chinese re-entry if they owned U.S. property valued at one thousand dollars or had a debt of like amount due them in the United States, did not appease the anti-Chinese lobbyists who were dissatisfied with the Gresham-Yang Treaty (Plates 45-46).

Whereas the United States dictated terms favorable to itself and American citizens continued to enjoy all rights and privileges in China, the same was denied the Chinese in the United States. The spirit of "reciprocity" was broken. These unfair and un-judicial acts towards the Chinese did not go unnoticed. Some fair-minded members of the press called attention to the fact that "...under treaty, they

[the Chinese] have just as much right to come here as we have to go to China" (Plate 47). In the same plate, both Republican and Democratic parties are seen as against Chinese immigration because with "no vote," the Chinese are of "no use to either party."

Similarly, Plate 48 satirizes the inequity of United States policies towards China. The Great Wall of China is broken down, permitting merchants and missionaries to enter, but simultaneously a wall of non-reciprocity, prejudice, un-American, jealousy, and law of race is built by American laborers to keep the Chinese out. These laborers consist of European immigrants and an African American. In "The Right Man in the Right Place" (Plate 49), the appointment of Senator Henry Blair as Minister to China is lampooned by the press as a joke. The administration of President Benjamin Harrison is criticized for its stupidity as the emperor of China is well aware of Minister Blair's prolific anti-Chinese speeches. In the end, China rejects Blair.

The last two cartoons bite further into American hypocrisy: In a Christian mission meeting, Chinese converts are collecting money to save the Americans from their own violence, prejudices, and corruption (Plate 50). Likewise in "The Ultimate Cause" (Plate 51), a Chinese Christian convert asks, "But why is it...that I may go to your heaven, while I may not go to your country?"

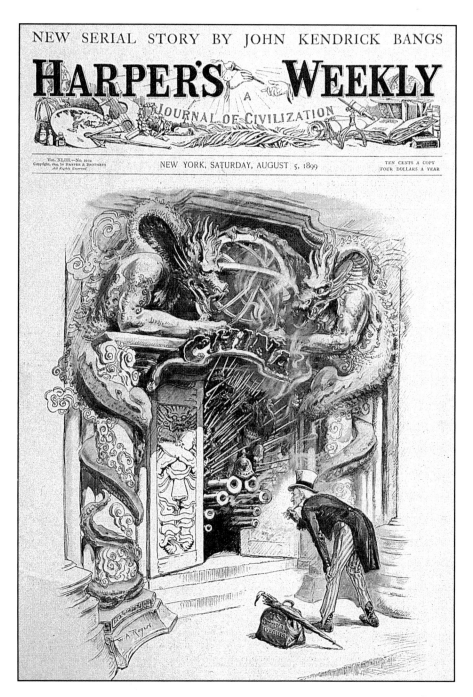

38   "The Open Door!"

39   A Fair Field and No Favor!
Uncle Sam:" I'm out for commerce, not conquest!"

40   The First Duty
Civilization (to China).—That dragon must be killed before our troubles can
be adjusted. If you don't do it I shall have to.

41   Reception of the Hon. Anson Burlingame and Members of the Chinese Embassy, by the Traveler's Club, May 30th 1868, at the Club House, 222 Fifth Avenue, New York City

42 California—Arrival at San Francisco of the First Resident Embassy of the Chinese Empire Accredited to the United States—Officers of the "Six Companies" Welcoming Chin Lan Pin and the Consular Corps in the Cabin of the "City of Tokio," July 25th

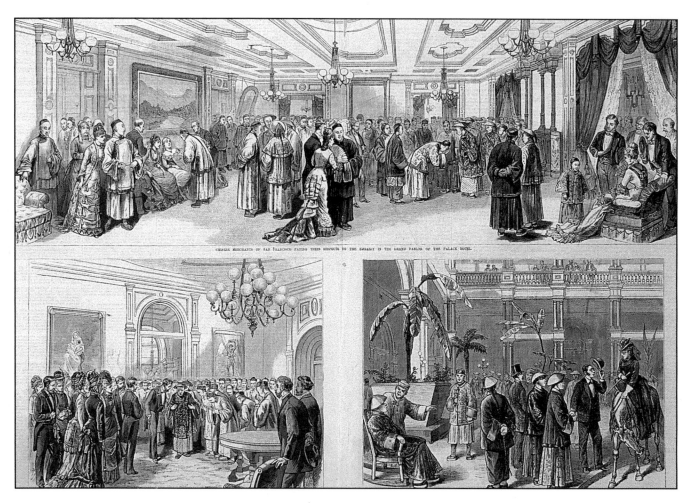

43   California—Arrival at San Francisco of the First Resident Embassy of the Chinese Empire Accredited to the United States, July 25th: (1) Chinese Merchants of San Francisco Paying Their Respects to the Embassy in the Grand Parlor of the Palace Hotel. (2) Arrival of the Embassy, Escorted by Resident Merchants at the Reception Saloon of the Hotel. (3) Members of the Embassy Promenading in the Lobby of the Hotel After Dining

44   The Chasm of Defeat Awaits His Uncertain Tread

45   "The Chinese Must Come."
Grover and Gresham Dallying with
Their Pets Once More

Chinese Minister: This one
velly good man—allee same one coolie.
Him owed a thousand dolla San
Flancisco. Him likee get in collect it.

Gresham: That's right. I'm in
favor of letting all like him in. Any good
Chinaman with an excuse should get in.
Me likee Chinaman allee same Cleveland. Bymeby I give you this key; open
gates whenever you like.

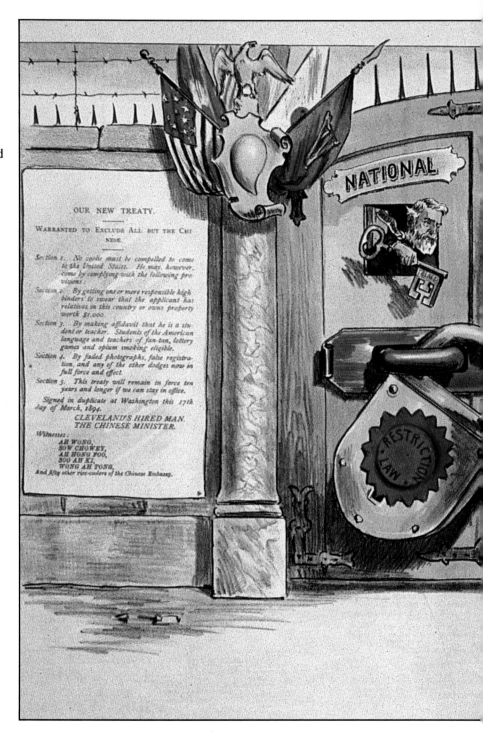

45

46   How They Will Evade the Chinese Treaty

What possible difference can it make to John Chinaman whether Democrats or Republicans have the upper hand? Both parties are his enemies. The advisability of preventing his coming or kicking out summarily those of him who are here, is a platform upon which both parties meet. We are not enamored of the Chinese; but so long as our merchants carry on business with them, under treaty, they have just as much right to come here as we have to go to China. No sophistry can alter this fact. The regular politicians, Dennis Kearney excepted, do not bother themselves much about the Chinese. Men without any votes are of no use; they would be better out of way, especially during a Presidential campaign. Perhaps it is a mistake not to permit them to become American citizens. They are surely as good as negroes, and quite as intelligent as a great many white men.

But neither candidate for President would have the temerity to advocate the cause of these Mongolians. It isn't a bit good for a campaign cry. We are sure that if Generals Hancock and Garfield had their way they would quietly collect all the Chinese and keep them at their own expense in the Mammoth Cave, at least until the election was over. This Chinese business is a very awkward one, and it always manages to crop up at an inopportune time. Perhaps, after all, the easiest way to get out of the difficulty is to give all Chinese notice to quit, and then for us to make up our minds for the future to dispense with the luxury of tea, fans, washee, and other things too numerous to particularize. We can eat a cake and have it too, nor must we expect to always have the sweets without an occasional dash of gall. [*Puck,* 14 July 1880, p. 336.]

47   Where Both Platforms Agree—No Vote—No Use to Either Party

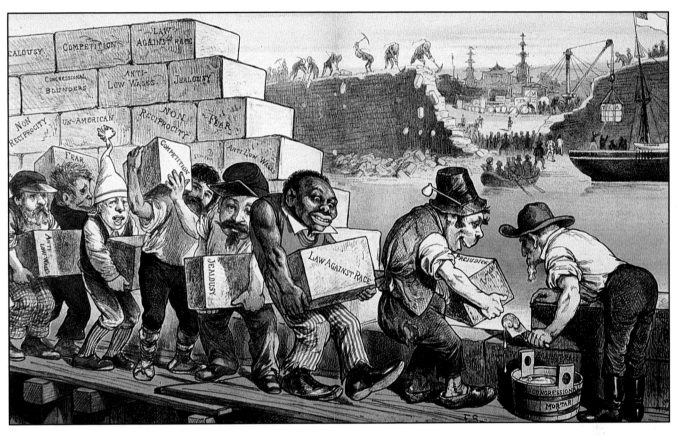

48   The Anti-Chinese Wall. The American Wall Goes Up as the Chinese Original Goes Down

There is one thing about the Harrison Administration that compels our admiration. When it sets out to be grotesque it puts the genius of the dime museums to the blush. When the public learned that Mr. Harrison had appointed Senator Blair to be Minister to China, there was a general disposition to credit the Pride of Indianapolis with a late development of a rudimentary sense of humor. To send to that particular post a man so narrow-minded, so pig-headed, so verbose, so thick-skinned and so unutterably tedious and empty and impracticable, generally, that even in the present Senate he was an object of especial ridicule—this certainly seemed like a practical joke—a joke in bad taste, but a joke, after its fashion. But when it was remembered that this same man had denounced the Chinese people in extravagant terms, and had advocated their exclusion from the United States, the joke was no longer a joke. It resolved itself into a characteristically Harrisonian monstrosity of bad judgement and indelicacy. [*Puck*, 11 March 1891, p. 34.]

49   The Right Man in the Right Place
The Emperor of China (to Minister Blair).—Welcome, Confucius of the Western World! We will have your speeches dramatized and played in nine hundred and ninety-seven acts and eighty-two tableaux.

50   As the Heathen See Us—A Meeting of the Chinese Missions Society

51   The Ultimate Cause
        "But why is it," asked the thoughtful Chinese, "that I may go to your heaven,
        while I may not go to your country?"
        The American missionary shrugged his shoulders. "There is no Labor vote in
        heaven!" said he.

Domestic Politics

III. DOMESTIC POLITICS

1. Labor versus Capital

As a young nation, the United States grew from an agrarian to an industrialized society. The Civil War also stimulated the expansion of large-scale manufacturing. Railroad promoters, iron producers, lumber kings, oil tycoons, and textile factory owners amassed financial fortunes while the people who actually produced the products were forced to work under degrading conditions for meager wages. Factory workers toiled from sun-up to sundown. In the textile mills, workers consisted of women and children under the age of twelve, working twelve to thirteen hours a day.

The conflict between capital and labor escalated (Plates 52-53). Ultimately, discontented workers revolted by forming labor unions to demand better working conditions and higher wages. Strikes and boycotts, oftentimes violent, were tactics used to force employers to grant improvements.

America's labor movement was engendered by the monopoly of capital and its exploitation of labor. On the West Coast, the Chinese became scapegoats in the growing pains of America's labor movement. Not only were the Chinese railroad builders but they were engaged in practically all branches of light industry. Henry George in his May 1, 1869 report to the *New York Tribune* summarized the situation:

The Chinese are rapidly monopolizing employment in all lighter branches of industry...such as running sewing machines, making paper boxes and bags, binding shoes, labelling and packing medicines....They are...used in grading railroads, cutting wood, picking fruit, tending stock...acting as firemen upon steamers, painting carriages, upholstering furniture, making boots, shoes, clothing, cigars, tin and wooden ware....

The Chinese were depicted as "many handed" or monstrous creatures depriving white laborers of their jobs (Plates 54-56). In patriotic calls, Americans were encouraged to boycott all Chinese-made products (Plate 57).

Anti-monopoly sentiment was very strong during the late

1800s and the Chinese without political influence became an easy target for hostility. The Big Four (Charles Crocker, Mark Hopkins, Collis P. Huntington, and Leland Stanford) were accused of railroad monopoly and controlling transportation in the West, and since they employed Chinese labor, the Chinese were also attacked as tools of the capitalists (Plates 58-60). Used as strike breakers against unions and in labor movements, the Chinese were depicted as an enemy of the working class. The fear of a Chinese takeover grew in the form of "cheap labor," which eventually became "The Chinese Question." Plate 61 (originally published in color) is *The Wasp*'s first anti-Chinese cartoon and clearly shows the white workingman's hostility towards the Chinese. Politicians who did not support the anti-Chinese movement were also castigated as enemies of the working class (Plates 62-63).

Among the many anti-Chinese groups that existed during the 1870s, Denis Kearney helped or-

ganized the Workingmen's Party of California in 1877, with the slogan, "The Chinese Must Go!" Kearney accused the Chinese of stealing jobs from white men and advocated Chinese exclusion. The party held many anti-Chinese meetings on the Sand Lots of San Francisco, some of which became violent. They cursed the railroads and they cursed the pro-Chinese politicians, but they attacked the Chinese (Plates 64-66).

The cry "The Chinese Must Go!" reverberated throughout the West Coast. Anti-Chinese associations were formed, mass meetings were held, riots were incited, and violence followed.

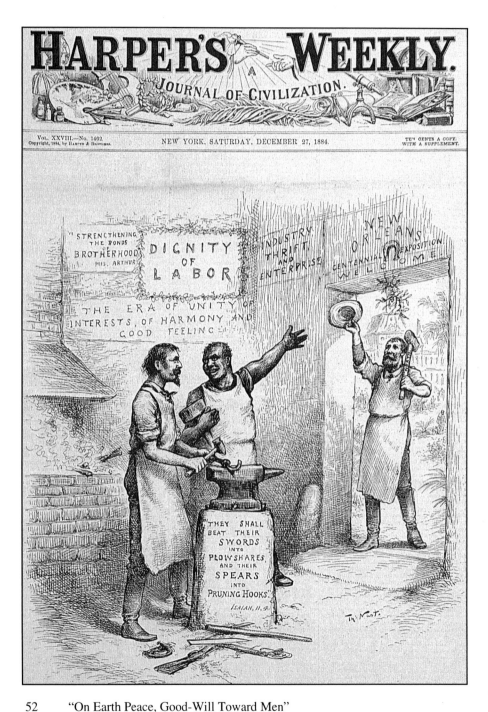

52   "On Earth Peace, Good-Will Toward Men"

53   Arbitration Is the True Balance of Power
       Puck.—Don't meddle with the hands, gentlemen—this pendulum is the
       only thing to regulate that clock!

54   What Shall We Do with Our Boys?

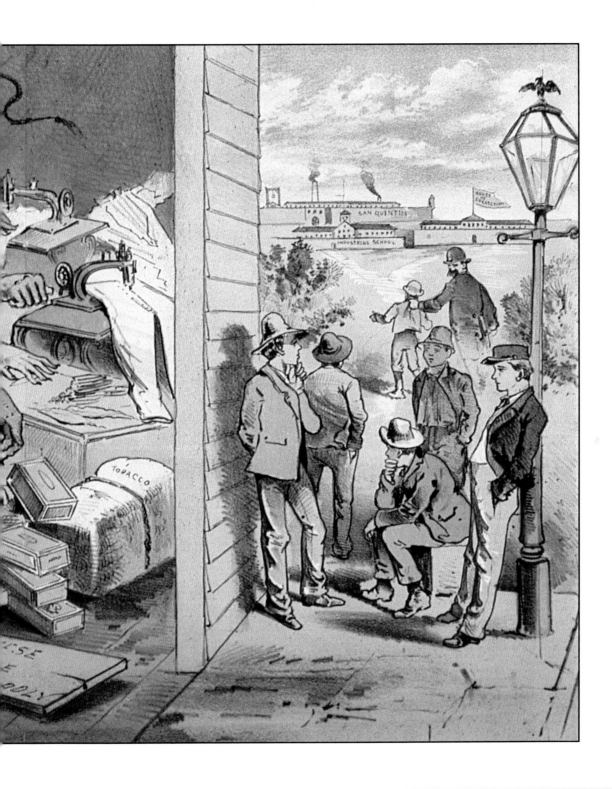

The all-absorbing character of Chinese competition is well illustrated in its many-handed god. On all sides it is reaching out for trades that it can master, and a crushing out of opposition is the inevitable result. Its Briarean arms stretch far and wide and crunch and rush out of existence every interest hostile to its monopoly. Our workingmen and women dependent upon their own hands and arms for support look with sad hearts upon this iconoclastic breaking down of all their employments, and in bitterness of soul cry aloud, "How long, O Lord, how long." [*The Wasp,* 14 November 1885, p. 6.]

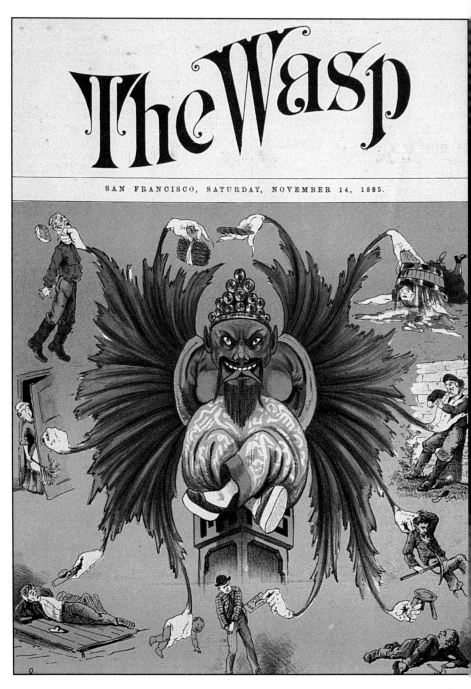

55   The Chinese: Many Handed But Soulless

Verily, the Pacific Coast has become the land of the tax-burdened and the home of the slave. With the transportation and the land in the hands of the few; with the Chinese and the Legislature, the party machines and the other afflictions, the most fruitful country on the face of the globe is fast becoming the most thriftless. The unsophisticated Mongol, imitating, ape-like, his fellow of this country, attains a monopoly of the cigar and laundry business, and smiles a cunning smile of triumph at his discomfited rivals. Centralization of money and of power in all departments of business is the rule, progressing daily in an increasing ratio. Our middle page has the misfortune to insinuate that the voting populace of California, in its entirety, is an ass [see Plate 60]. The insinuation would be unfortunate if it were not true. As long as the voters of the State are willing to sit quietly by, submitting to the dominance of a political machinery that retains in power the sources of present ills, just so long may they expect to be badly governed and robbed in the tax levy. [*The Wasp,* 20 May 1881, p. 322.]

56   The Coming Man
      Allee samee 'Melican Man Monopoleeee.

~·HEADQUARTERS·~

OF THE

Boot and Shoemakers' White Labor League,

SHOEMAKERS' HALL,　　597 MISSION ST.

SAN FRANCISCO, CALIFORNIA.

TO THE MEMBERS OF THE FARMERS' ALLIANCE OF CALIFORNIA:

GREETING: We, the members of the Boot and Shoe Makers' White Labor League, beg leave to call your attention to the resolution passed by your State Executive Committee at their meeting held in San Francisco January 11, 1891, as follows:

" We hereby recommend an early conference with our State Business Manager in order to settle the preliminary steps necessary to be taken, and under his direction we will use all reasonable measures to aid in extending the work and influence of the Boot and Shoemakers' White Labor League of our State."

You will be aiding the White Shoemakers of our State by buying the goods made by them, and our White Labor League Stamp, impressed plainly on the bottom of every pair, is the only proof and guaranty of their being the production of white mechanics.

All Boots or Shoes bearing this Stamp are made of whole stock, without shoddy, and will wear better than any other sold at the same price.

Therefore, you will readily see that it will not only be CHEAPER for you to buy Boots and Shoes bearing the White Labor League Stamp, but you will at the same time be helping the White Shoemakers of this city and State to support themselves and families. The Stamp of the Boot and Shoe Makers' White Labor League (a fac simile of which appears at the head of this circular,) has been issued to twelve different manufacturers, who employ about 1000 men and 700 girls, representing a total of over 5000 people depending on this industry for their livelihood.

No manufacturer using this Stamp is permitted to employ Chinese in the making of Boots or Shoes, and for this reason our Stamp on a Boot or Shoe is the only positive proof that it was made by White Labor

Address all communications to

ALEXIS SULLIVAN,

General Secretary Boot and Shoemakers' White Labor League.

☞ **Please keep this for reference.**

57　　　Boot and Shoemakers' White Labor League

58   Swords of Damocles

"Anti-Monopoly" is the political war cry of America in the future. Already it has been sounded bravely in New York, and its ring has been caught up and echoed in every State of the Union. The party is forming in this city. Throughout the interior of this State a great army of voters only wait for the call to arraign themselves, irrespective of party feeling, irrespective of all other public ties, in the line that is advancing against the common enemy. The Anti-Monopoly party in this State will be a tremendously successful one. The promise is so good that the shrewdest political managers will take hold of it, and in their own interest push it forward in a smooth path which the past has made ready for it. San Francisco has thousands of voters to whom the question needs but to be deftly put (for there are two sides to it) to gain thousands of converts and voters. The State, from Siskiyou to San Bernardino, is in bitter hostility to the Railroad. If proof be needed, the passage of the new Constitution, in the face of grand obstacles, is sufficient. Its racial quality will make the movement acceptable to thousands not directly interested, but desirous, as the successful class in every community always is, of "a change." So we predict for the Anti-Monopoly party a grand success. That it should succeed is to be hoped, for the time has already arrived when the great monopolies, with their limitless funds, their control of legislatures and their ramification of power, are more powerful than the United States Government itself. And nothing, save a grand powerful campaign against them can check their growth or weaken their power—if even that can—entrenched as they are in Court and Capital all over the Union. [*The Wasp,* 9 April 1881, p. 226.]

59   The Modern St. George

60   When Will This Ass Kick
        A case for the Society for Prevention of Cruelty to Animals.

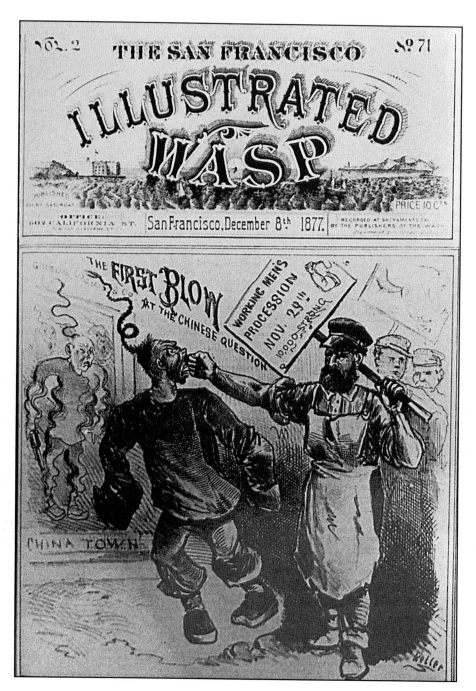

61   The First Blow at the Chinese Question

VOL. XIV.-No. 339.   SEPTEMBER 5, 1883.   Price, 10 Cents.

"What fools these Mortals be!"
MIDSUMMER-NIGHTS DREAM.

Puck

PUBLISHED BY
KEPPLER & SCHWARZMANN.   NEW YORK   OFFICE No. 21-23 WARREN ST.
TRADE MARK REGISTERED 1878
"ENTERED AT THE POST OFFICE AT NEW YORK, AND ADMITTED FOR TRANSMISSION THROUGH THE MAILS AT SECOND CLASS RATES"

62   A Trio That Must Go

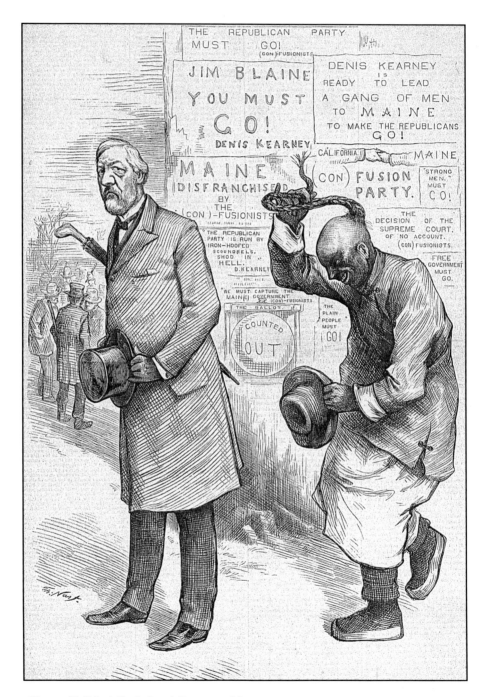

63   Political Capital and Compound Interest
Non-Voter. "Now Melican Man know muchee how it is himself."

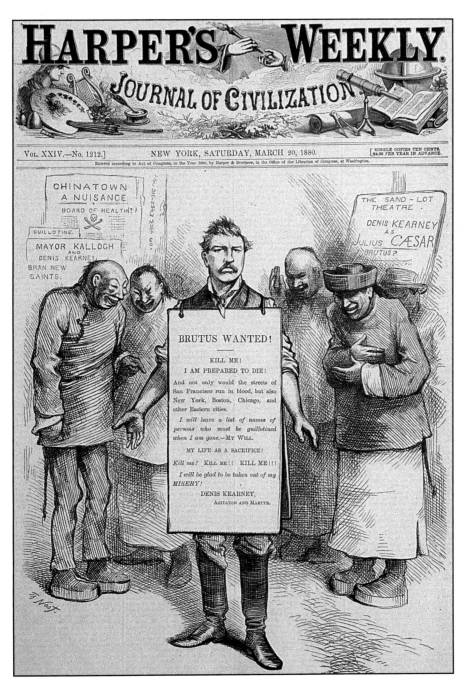

64   The Ides of March
        Don't—Put Him Out of His Misery.

65   California—The Chinese Agitation in San Francisco—A Meeting of the Workingmen's Party on the Sand Lots

66   The New Comet—A Phenomenon Now Visible in All Parts of the United States

2. Yellow Peril Propaganda

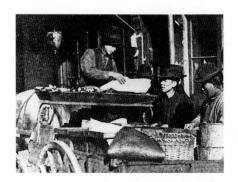

The perception "white is superior" was widely shared by members of the press. In Plate 67, "The Pigtail Has Got to Go," the United States represents the advanced civilization cutting off the queue representing China's decadence or "worn-out traditions." From the acid inked pen of editors and political cartoonists came the scathing, condescending, and foulest kind of racism. The population was forewarned of the Chinese "invasion" and foretold of its consequences.

This section on Yellow Peril propaganda is subdivided into three categories to show how political cartoons were used to create fear and hatred of the Chinese: cartoons that illustrate the cultural inferiority of the Chinese in order to justify white supremacy; cartoons depicting interracial relations between the Chinese and other ethnic minorities, some of which functioned to create division among the various ethnic groups; and cartoons of prediction to describe what would happen if there were a Chinese takeover.

Cultural Inferiority. White supremacy, encouraged by white man's claim of a "manifest destiny" to inherit the riches of America, viewed all other races to be culturally, mentally, and physically inferior. The Chinese were no exception. Believing the Chinese to be inferior, editors and political cartoonists with malice, ridiculed them as cultural inferiors, physically grotesque, morally depraved, and carriers of the deadliest diseases. For example, the presence of the bubonic plague was a deliberate scare fabricated by the Board of Health in a campaign to convince San Franciscans of the necessity to get rid of the Chinese and to burn Chinatown (Plate 68). Vices were sensationalized and attributed to the Chinese: gambling, opium smoking, prostitution, and the debauchery of white women (Plates 69-73). Chinese women or "Celestial ladies" were caricatured as having "baboon-like faces" (Plate 74). Satirizing Darwin's theory on evolution, the Chinese evolves from a monkey and then evolves into a pig (Plate 75). Presenting the Chinese in a subhuman and immoral manner helped to justify racism and furthered the cause of anti-Chinese lobbyists.

67   The Pigtail Has Got to Go

68   The Bubonic Plague in San Francisco. Chinamen, Confined Within the
      Chinese Quarter, Cooking Their Meals

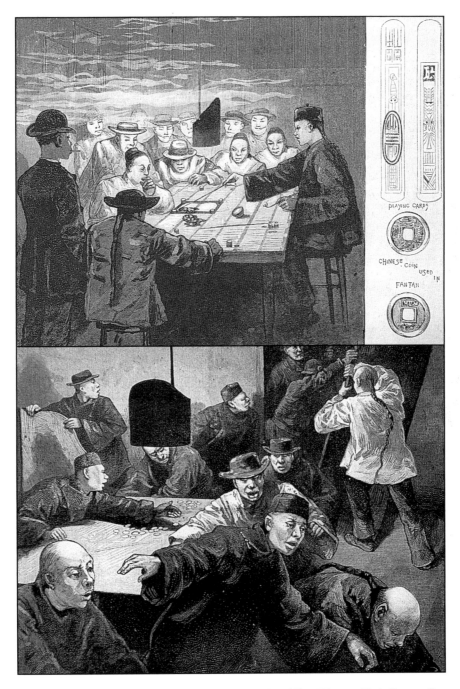

73   New York City—Scenes in a Chinese Gambling-House. (1) A Game of
        "Fan-Tan" in Progress. (2) A Raid by the Police

Interracial Conflict. In the racist climate that prevailed, it was a foregone conclusion among nativists that white was superior to color. This racist approach was further applied to determine who shall or shall not be an American. Europeans were more desirable than the Chinese (Plates 44; 76-77) and the Chinese were ranked undesirable along with Native and African Americans. In some cases, the Chinese were even less desirable (Plate 78), especially when the Chinese had no vote (Plate 79).

Political cartoonist Thomas Nast was well aware of the prejudices and discrimination, and satirized this in the South, "The Nigger Must Go" and in the West, "The Chinese Must Go" (Plate 80). In his "Every Dog Has His Day" (Plate 81), the Red Gentleman (almost annihilated) explains to the perplexed Yellow Gentleman why he must go: "Pale face 'fraid you crowd him out, as he did me." Meanwhile, an African American is waiting for his day. Fair play and protection for the Chinese is portrayed by Miss Columbia protecting the Chinese from the angry mob (Plate 82). Finally, in Nast's illustration of "Uncle Sam's Thanksgiving Dinner" (Plate 83), the artist envisioned an American family "free and equal." The open invitation "come one come all" even included a Chinese family. His version was idealistic if not realistic.

In the "war of races," the Chinese were pitted against Irish and African Americans. Whereas the West (Irish) demanded the Chinese to go, the South wanted the Chinese to come and replace the African Americans (Plate 84). Plate 85 shows Chinese laundrymen already displacing the "colored washerwomen." The Irish, occupying the end of the social ladder amongst European immigrants, competed with the Chinese for menial jobs (Plate 86). In this plate, America's China policy is blamed for inducing the Chinese to the shores of Manhattan Island. Miss Columbia tosses life preservers (treaty obligations, etc.) to save drowning rats that slowly evolve into Chinese as they reach the shore. In this political cartoon, the Irish have no use for the Chinese just as the Chinese are depicted holding an "Irish Must Go" rally.

Fear and jealousy among ethnic groups made unity difficult especially when other ethnic minorities looked upon the Chinese as a threat to their own economic well being. The oppressed victim becomes the scapegoat responsible for the nation's racism and ills. This divide-and-conquer manipulation of animosity among racial groups helped those in power retain their position of power.

76   An Altered Course

77   The Chinaman's Idea of It
        "Allee litee, Melican man wantee suchee pleople for votee, Chinaman no wantee stayee. He go wilout being toldee."

78   Be Just—Even to John Chinaman

Judge (to Miss Columbia), "You allowed that boy to come into your school, it would be inhuman to throw him out now—it will be sufficient in the future to keep his brothers out!"

79   The Civilization of Blaine
        John Confucius, "Am I not a Man and a Brother?"

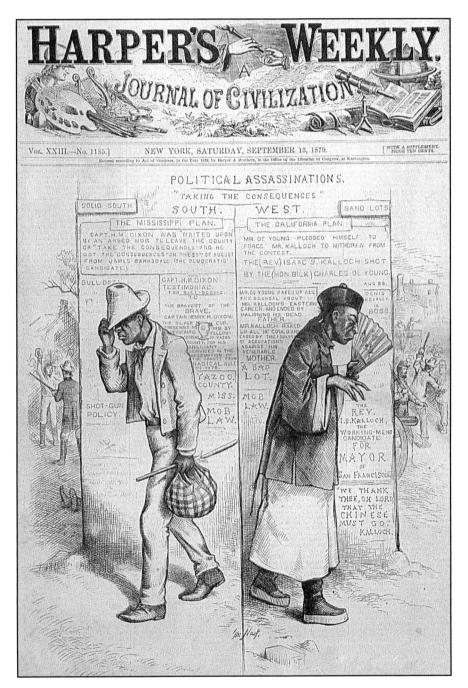

80　　　"The Nigger Must Go," and "The Chinese Must Go"
The Poor Barbarians Can't Understand Our Civilized Republican Form of
Government.

81   "Every Dog" (No Distinction of Color) "Has His Day"
        Red Gentleman to Yellow Gentleman, "Pale face 'fraid you crowd him
        out, as he did me."

84   What Shall We Do with John Chinaman?
        What Pat Would Do with Him. What Will Be Done with Him.

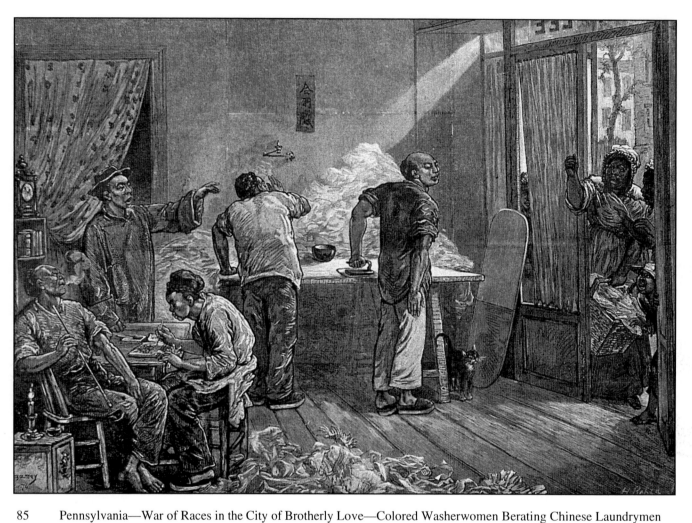

85   Pennsylvania—War of Races in the City of Brotherly Love—Colored Washerwomen Berating Chinese Laundrymen

86   The Chinese Invasion

Predictions. America was forewarned if the Chinese "invasion" was not stopped, "The Consequences of Coolieism" would result in the ruination of the American family: the father commits suicide, the son is caught stealing bread, the mother is in despair, and the daughter is hooked on opium (Plate 87). Likewise, if the "Chinese Tiger" continues his "growth from subserviency and weakness to the tiger-like spirit of fierce power and destruction which characterizes the Chinese laborer," it will be the end of America (Plate 88).

The war of the races is inevitable in P.W. Dooner's 1880 novel, *Last Days of the Republic*. When America is defeated in the end, a Chinese Mandarin takes over as governor of California and Mandarin politicians govern the nation from Washington, D.C. (Plates 89-93). Plate 94 further predicts America's "Fourth." A celebratory parade takes place on San Francisco's Market Street and is passing in front of the Palace Hotel on 2nd Street. Here the role of subserviency is reversed: one white man sells Chinese newspaper while another is the laundryman; a white barber gives the Chinese a haircut; a white cabby drives for Chinese passengers; and a Chinese policeman is arresting a white pauper.

With the Chinese "invasion," Chinese men would take over "our" white women (Plate 95), Miss Columbia would be nursing Chinese babies (Plate 96), and the statue for "our" harbor would be a "Chinaman" holding an opium pipe (Plate 97). For some thirty years, predictions that a Chinese takeover meant the end of morality and civilization occupied the politics of the West Coast. The answer to their "Chinese Question" was clear: "The Coming Man" must go!

87   Consequences of Coolieism

But it is not alone in the field of labor that the evils of the Asiatic interloper are felt. He is the ruin of the household. Our artist has pictured on the last page a panorama of distress which is by no means a work of imagination. The wreck of the white workingman's family is graphically depicted. The leering, idiotic and immodest attitude of the daughter of the house shows the damning influence of the opium-pipe; the father, driven from employment, despairingly seeks relief in a suicide's death, leaving his widow destitute, famished and despondent; the son, driven to stealing bread for himself and mother, finds himself a felon. In the clutches of the law; while near by in a huge manufactory may be seen the cause of all the evil in the fact that Chinese are driving the white men from employment, hurling them from the windows and kicking them out of the doors. Surely such a spectacle must stir the blood in the veins of either Saxon or Celt. [*The Wasp,* 7 November 1885, p. 3.]

The aggressive spirit shown by the Chinese in our midst during the last week has thoroughly aroused this city to a sense of the danger by which we are environed. At first tolerated and even nourished as a desirable labor element the little brown man has assiduously burrowed at the foundations of manufacturing enterprise until he has wormed himself into a commanding position in many of our industrial pursuits. No sooner does he feel his power and calculate that he is boss of the situation than all of his assumed subserviency forsakes him and he reveals his natural bent of tyranny. The spectacle of seventy Chinese cigar-makers in one factory striking from work and refusing to longer labor unless eighty-eight white men in the same establishment should first be discharged, is such an exhibition of arrogant impudence that it has opened the eyes of our people to the evil that we have been breeding. The laborer that first came to our shores, docile, humble and tractable, has been growing stronger in his position day by day under the nurture of employment until at last feeling impregnable to competition he asserts himself as the monopolist of labor and the destroyer of his employers' trade. Not until this latest exhibition of his domineering character would our people believe that such an evil impended. It is now plain to their widely-opened eyes that an irrepressible conflict between the Chinaman and the white workingman exists and is being worked out to the destruction of one or the other. Which shall go to the wall? Should the answer be doubtful when the solution of the problem is in our hands? Can it be that white men will aid, assist, support and nourish the open, avowed and powerful enemy of their own race? Is there not a spirit of patriotism in every man's breast sufficient to induce him to reject the work of the heathen and accept instead the goods manufactured by his own people? Is not our own race and civilization worthy our preference, and will not Americans see to it that the arrogance of the now insolent Mongol shall be curbed—and for all time? Surely no argument should be needed in the premises. The instincts of every white man should prompt him to immediate and complete repudiation of all Chinese-made goods, in favor of our own countrymen. If this be unanimously adopted and honestly carried out the problem of Chinese competition will be solved. Our own workingmen will be the more prosperous, happy and contented in consequence and the moon-eyed stranger must go to his lair. He would thus be driven to his "far-away Cathay" and this too without a return-certificate. Such a course would be equal to any restriction act that can be passed, even to entire exclusion. Our double-page cartoon is intended to show the lesson of gradual growth from subserviency and weakness to the tiger-like spirit of fierce power and destruction which characterizes the Chinese laborer. [*The Wasp,* 7 November 1885, p. 3.]

88   In the Clutches of the Chinese Tiger

89   The Ship of State Glided Noiselessly to Her Doom

90   The Beginning of the End

89-93   Last Days of the Republic

Meantime the conquerors had entered the Capital. The Republic had fought its last battle; and the Imperial Dragon of China already floated from the dome of the Capitol.

The very name of the United States of America was thus blotted from the record of nations and peoples, as unworthy the poor boon of existence. Where once the proud domain of forty States, besides millions of miles of unorganized territory, cultivated the arts of peace and gave to the world its brightest gems of literature, art and scientific discovery, the Temple of Liberty had crumbled; and above its ruins was reared the colossal fabric of barbaric splendor known as the Western Empire of his August Majesty the Emperor of China and Ruler of all lands.

Forever occupied and diverted by its factions and its politicians, in their local intrigues for the acquisition of political power, the Ship of State sailed proudly on, too blinded by her preoccupation and too reliant in her strength to bestow a thought upon the perils of the sea. She sighted afar the foam of the maelstrom, and tossed her haughty pennants in sovereign disdain of its power. But its current was around her, and she glided unconsciously to her doom. In vain the exercise of her giant strength; in vain that her factions, in happy forgetfulness of their petty antipathies, united their powers to save! Too late! She was hurled, helpless and struggling, to ruin and annihilation; and as she sank, engulfed, she carried with her the prestige of a race; for in America the representatives of the one race of man, which, in its relation to the family of men, had borne upon its crest the emblem of sovereign power since the dawn of history, saw now the ancestral diadem plucked from its proud repose, to shed its lustre upon an alien crown. Thus passed away the glory of the Union of States, at the dawn of the Twentieth Century. [P.W. Dooner, *Last Days of the Republic* (San Francisco: Alta California Publishing House, 1880), pp.256-258.]

91   The War of the Races

92   The Mandarins in Washington

93   The Governor of California

94   The "Fourth" of the Future

95   Pacific Railroad Complete

96   The Last Addition to the Family

97   A Statue for Our Harbor

3. Anti-Chinese Riots

As the conflict between labor and capital increased, Yellow Peril rhetoric and propaganda intensified. Anti-Chinese meetings were followed oftentimes by riots in which Chinese communities were firebombed and people murdered. One such meeting held in San Francisco on March 4, 1882, was declared a legal holiday by California Governor George C. Perkins, and was supported by both the Democratic and Republican parties (Plate 98). The claim that Chinese labor displaces white labor was a volatile issue ready to explode any second (Plate 99). Mass riots erupted throughout the West: from Washington Territory (Black Diamond, Newcastle, Puyallup, Olympia, Seattle, Issaquah Valley, Tacoma, etc.) to the state of California (Chico, Eureka, Hollister, Humbolt County, Los Angeles, Merced, Pasadena, Redding, Truckee, Vacaville, Wheatland, Yuba County, etc.). Many Chinese kicked out of cities sought refuge in San Francisco's Chinatown. Four years after the 1882 Chinese Ex-

clusion Act, San Francisco found itself the "dumping ground of the entire country" with no help from the state or federal government to handle the influx of Chinese kicked out from the other American communities (Plate 100).

In October 1880, a riot erupted in Denver, Colorado, when three thousand white men attacked four hundred Chinese, destroying Chinatown and killing a Chinese laundryman (Plate 101). Property loss was estimated at $53,655. Minister Chen Lanbin demanded the imprisonment of the guilty parties plus compensation for property losses suffered by the Chinese victims. Secretary of State William M. Evarts and President Rutherford Hayes expressed regret and anger, but said in accordance with the Constitution, the federal government could not interfere with municipal laws. Chen argued on the basis that this case should be resolved between China and the United States under treaty terms. When James G. Blaine took over as Secretary of State in 1881, Blaine

upheld the Constitution as the supreme law of the United States and stated that America was not liable by way of any Sino-American treaties for the losses suffered by the Chinese in Denver.

The September 1855 Rock Springs riot in Wyoming was better known as a massacre because twenty-eight Chinese miners were

killed, fifteen wounded, and several hundred chased out of town (Plate 102). An estimated $147,000 worth of Chinese property was destroyed. This time, Chinese Minister Zheng Zaoru formally presented Secretary of State Thomas Francis Bayard, Sr., with a letter to negotiate indemnity for the Denver and Rock Springs victims (Plates 103-104). Bayard's official reply did not hold the United States government liable, but recommended that Congress make some compensation as a goodwill posture. On February 24, 1887, the Chinese Indemnity Bill was passed for $147,748.74, per the amount requested by the Chinese to the penny.

The Seattle riot occurred one month after the Rock Springs massacre (Plate 105). Three Chinese were killed and three were wounded by white men. All the Chinese homes were burned. Chinese Consul General Ouyang Ming in San Francisco cabled Governor Watson C. Squire to protect the Chinese from further assault. The situation worsened when several

days later, hundreds of Chinese were driven from nearby Tacoma and Puyallup, with Chinese merchants given one day to pack and leave. The governor requested federal aid and President Grover Cleveland immediately ordered federal troops into Tacoma and Seattle to suppress the riots. This was considered the first time the federal government took an active role in protecting its Chinese residents.

98 "The Mountain in Labor" (Aesop's Fables)

99 Will It Come to This?

100   San Francisco. Must I Support Them All?

Our artist has given us a signifi-cant phase of the Chinese question, which is just now of controlling interest to this city. It is all very well for the rest of the country to get rid of their Chinamen, but what of forcing them all upon us. San Francisco sits supinely under the domina-tion of the Chinese Six Companies, and concerts measures to counteract the evils of the Chinese competition already here, when suddenly she finds herself the dump-ing ground of the entire country. They come on foot, by steamer, in railway cars, on wagons and almost seem to descend from balloons and to come up out of the sea. There is no end to their multiplication in our midst. What is to be done with them? We cannot drive them out as smaller communities have done. There is no place to drive them to, and the State and Federal Government both would prevent violence if threatened against the intruders. Under these circumstances poor San Francisco can only "suffer and be strong" and pursue the policy of letting the "little brown man" severely alone. In other words, he must be starved out, and perhaps this can better be done by having more of him than less. He will thus the sooner eat himself out of substance. [*The Wasp,* 27 February 1886, p. 3.]

101   Colorado—The Anti Chinese Riot in Denver, on October 31st

4. Exclusion Politics

The period of free migration to the United States for Chinese laborers ended with the 1880 Angell Treaty and the 1882 Chinese Exclusion Act. During the 1880 treaty negotiations, China under the Manchu government was a powerless nation. The United States was able to pressure the Chinese to voluntarily restrict its citizens from leaving for America. Taking further advantage, Congress tried to pass Senate Bill 71 introduced by Senator John F. Miller to exclude the entry of Chinese laborers for twenty years (Plate 106). However, President Rutherford B. Hayes acknowledged the goodwill between the two countries under the Burlingame Treaty and vetoed the exclusion. When Vice President Chester A. Arthur became president upon President James A. Garfield's death, Congress tried again to pass the same act. At first President Arthur vetoed it on the grounds that a twenty-year exclusionary period was excessive and in violation of the 1880 Treaty (Plate 107). This prompted Congress to reduce the years to ten. Subsequently, in his bid for election to stay as president and under pressure from national labor organizations, President Arthur signed the Act of May 6, 1882, commonly known as the Chinese Exclusion Act. The act stated that it was "the opinion of the Government of the United States the coming of Chinese laborers to this country endangers the good order of certain localities within the territory thereof," and should therefore be suspended for the next ten years.

When ten years passed, an anti-Chinese Congress consisting of both Democrats and Republicans proposed over twelve bills to extend the exclusion. California Congressman Thomas J. Geary authored the Geary Act which was signed by President Benjamin Harrison on May 5, 1892, to suspend Chinese immigration for another ten years. Chinese Minister Tsui Kwoyin [Cui Guoyin] strongly protested on the grounds that the Geary Act violated the 1880 treaty, but the United States government

ignored him.

In 1902, Chinese merchants in San Francisco urged Chinese Minister Wu Tingfang to warn the United States Congress about extending the exclusion another time. Wu also threatened the boycotting

of American goods as a form of retaliation. In total disregard of the Chinese, the April 29, 1902 Act signed into law by President Theodore Roosevelt not only continued the exclusionary policy but also prohibited Chinese immigration to all territories under the jurisdiction of the United States. Chinese exclusion was eventually extended indefinitely in the General Deficiency Appropriations Account Act of 1904. The anger felt by the Chinese was visible in both America and China. A nationwide boycott campaign against the United States erupted in China in May 1905.

    In the process of negotiating treaties and drafting the exclusion laws, those diplomats and politicians who conceded the slightest compromise to the Chinese were castigated. When President Arthur first failed to sign the Chinese exclusion bill, he was caricatured as a mother "amusing the baby" (the anti-Chinese constituents) while a menacing household pet in the image of a sinister half-dragon, half-Chinese watches with satisfaction (Plate 108). Those politicians who were pro-China trade were singled out and ridiculed as subservient by kowtowing to the Chinese, and were degraded by wearing Chinese clothes and adopting the "pigtail" (Plates 109-112). In Plate 113, they are seen outwitted by the "Heathen Chinee."

    While the exclusionists were successful in abrogating the Burlingame Treaty and enacting exclusion laws, they were far from victorious in their battle for total exclusion and expulsion of the Chinese from American soil. In spite of the numerous laws, the Chinese found loopholes. Following the passage of the 1882 Exclusion Act, the Chinese came through British Columbia with British certificates of entry. The image of hordes of Chinese thus circumventing the exclusion acts horrified the exclusionists (Plates 114-115).

    Furthermore, returning Chinese laborers were permitted to re-enter if they had $1,000 value of assets and/or a wife and child in the United States (see Sino-American Relations, Plates 45-46). Those who were denied re-entry to the United States jammed the courts with writs of *habeas corpus*. Judge Sawyer of the United States Circuit Court, in his ruling on *habeas corpus* cases, was accused of accepting bribery and making millions by dumping "millions" of Chinese into California (Plate 116).

    The complexity of exclusion politics is summarized in the article appearing with Plate 117, "The Restriction Act Kicked Out." In a baseball game, the anti-Chinese team is pitted against their rival pro-Chinese team.

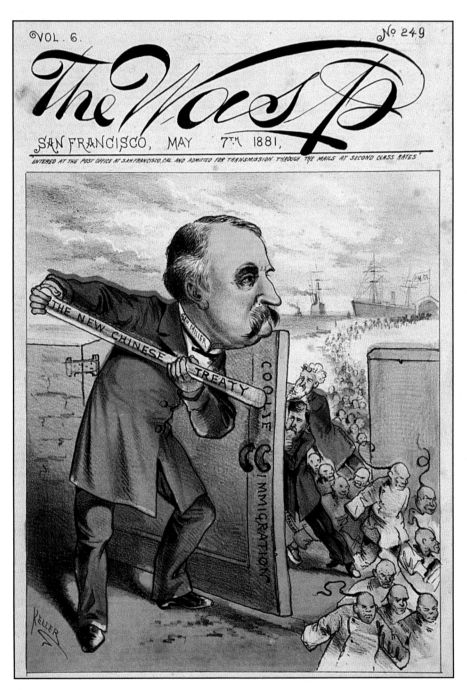

106   Hard Pushing

The objection of the President and his supporters to the twenty years' limit of the Chinese restrictive bill is that the whole bill is of the nature of an experiment, and it would not be prudent to bind ourselves for so long a period to its continuance. If this is not idle nonsense we really do not know what to call it. Cannot Congress at any time repeal the act or modify it in any of its provisions? If it had become a law with the twenty years provision, and at the end of ten years it should have been found to be working mischief, nothing could have been easier than to repeal it, enacting a new law to meet the new requirements or enacting none at all. No new treaty with China would be necessary, for the treaty now in force does not require, but only permits, us to suspend immigration. But the bill was not truly experimental at all, for at the end of twenty years, or ten years, or five years of suspension we shall be no better able to judge of its effect upon our material welfare than we now are to forecast it. The problem is complicated with too many factors, and it will be beyond the powers of human intelligence to say with any confidence what part the exclusion of Chinese labor has had in quickening our industries and augmenting our prosperity—just as it now is impossible to say with certainty how much it has done in the other direction. We are now all confident that it is an evil; if we are right its absence will be always a blessing; if wrong, no misfortunes caused by its suspension will convict us of present error, so long as we are free to attribute them to other causes. All the same, we shall have to defer to the President's views and provide for reopening the whole question some years hence, with no new light and a possibly adverse Congress. [*The Wasp*, 14 April 1882.]

107   His Hands Tied
"Who Governs Freemen Should Himself Be Free."

108   Amusing the Child

A tempest in a teapot has been raging the past week on account of a fanciful insult to a Chinese embassy that landed at this port. The law provides that the "credentials" of such magnates shall admit them to the United States; and that no other papers or certificate shall be required. Such being the case, the Collector of the Port, under that spirit of courtesy which permeates international comity, permitted the distinguished guests to land without even the formality of an inspection of their official authority. In mild unconsciousness of any wrong done he pursued the even tenor of his way, knowing that the law was his rule of action; when lo and behold! a storm of administrative indignation came on the lightning's wing, and let him to understand that the Cabinet was in commotion over complaints made against him by the Chinese authorities. Our Secretary of State had gone off in a fever of spluttering indignation, and prostrated himself and his authority at the feet of the Mongolian, while the President was shaking with aspen quiverings of fear lest a spirit of retaliation should murder every white man in China. Since sober reason and the facts in the premises have assumed sway it is found that Judge Hager has done but his full duty in the premises, and that our Washington authorities have unnecessarily demeaned themselves in the presence of the Mandarins of the East. [*The Wasp,* 17 April 1886, p. 6.]

109   Laws Rules Here—Diplomacy at Washington

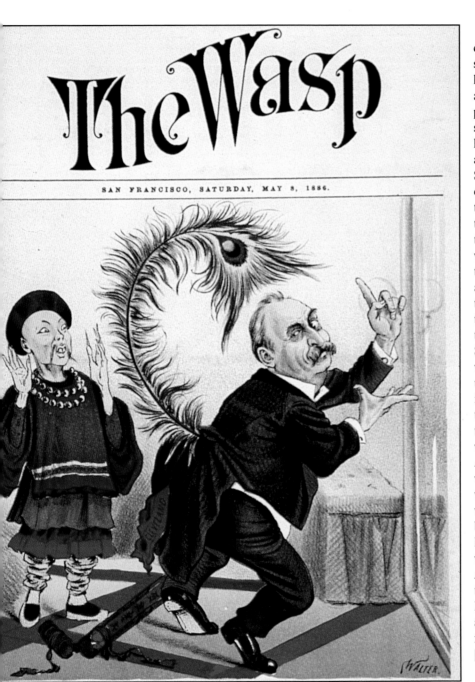

The Wasp

SAN FRANCISCO, SATURDAY, MAY 8, 1886.

110   President Cleveland's Reward for Subserviency

What's the matter with our President, anyhow? He bows and cringes at the shrine of the Chinese Mandarins as though he feared the presence of their hostile fleet at our seaport entrance, and felt bound to placate their resentment at any cost of spirit and manhood. It was not enough for him to send a special message to Congress all but commanding it to divert the United States Treasury to payment of Chinese claims; but he must in addition protest to the Chinese minister against his own countrymen; asseverate the desire of this nation to be on terms of friendly intimacy with almond-eyed strangers—whereas in truth the less we see of them the better—and generally prostrate the government at the feet of the Mongolian in servile imitation of a second or third class power. And to what end—what does he get in return? Some idle platitudes of diplomacy whose vitality is as ephemeral as the breath that utters them. What we want in this business is to tell China plainly—by treaty or statutory enactment—that we claim this country for ourselves and our children and that we want the Chinese to remain at home. As to trade, if we have anything they want we will sell it, and if they have anything we want we will buy it. There never yet was individual or nation that would not do business on these terms. As to the Chinese here, if we let them severely alone they will soon find more congenial quarters. All this dancing of obeisance at the call of the Celestial stranger on the part of our President and Cabinet is humiliating to us as a first class nation, and as childish as the flutter of feather or the tickling of a straw. [*The Wasp,* 8 May 1886, p. 3.]

111   The Adoration of the 6,000-Year-Old Chinese Idea, and If Its Disciples Keep
       It Up Long Enough, They Will Surely Bring Us All to Eating Rats and Rice

112   The Burning Question

113   Ah Sam Randall, The Heathen Chinee

114   The Last Load

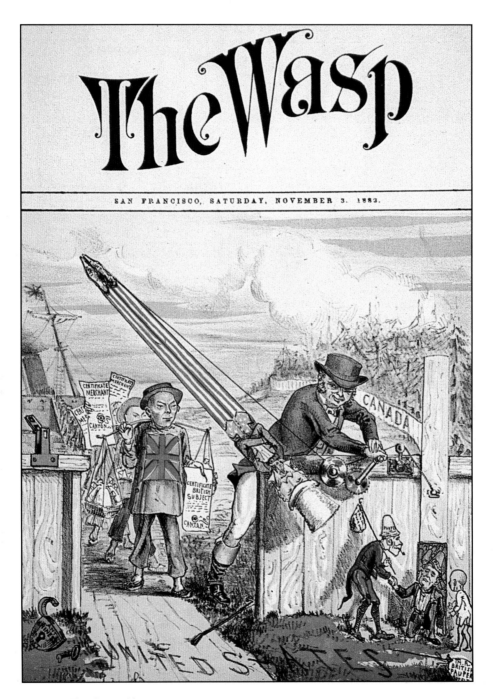

115   The Gates Ajar

116   There's Millions in It

117   The Restriction Act Knocked Out

In our double-page cartoon is an allegorical representation of one phase of the Chinese question. Representing a baseball game between the civic authorities and the Asiatics, we have Senator Miller pitching the ball (the Restriction Act) at the Chinaman on the home plate. Collector-of-Customs Sears stands behind and is earnestly determined to "catch him out." The Mongol, however, defeats this purpose, for with his gnarled and misshapen "bat" of Perjury he negatives the efforts of both pitcher and catcher and sends the ball "skywards" over the fence into the Supreme Court. This being out of the bounds, the Act is a "lost ball," and will so remain until in the slowness of revolving years the Federal judiciary chooses to return it. United States Judge Sawyer acts as Referee between the parties, but owing to the sinuosities, bends and curves of the telescopic law through which he is compelled to look he has entirely lost sight of the ball. Surveyor-of-the-Port Morton, whose business it is to be the first man on incoming ships and deny a landing to any Chinaman who has not a proper certificate, in this pictured game acts as "short-stop" and is frantic in his efforts to cut short the ball in its aerial flight. But the Chinaman has sent it over his head. United States District-Attorney Hilborn finding that the Mongols have beaten the "pitcher," the "catcher" and the "short-stop," and are passing all the "bases," in turn, puts himself in the way as the expositor of the law to prevent a "home-run," but he finds himself toppled over and knocked out of line by a "habeas corpus," which the almond-eyed stranger always applies as a last resort. Thus he makes the goal of a home landing, and an interminable line of his fellows under the intelligent "coaching" of Colonel Bee, their captain, awaits in turn the running of the "corners." A Pacific Mail steamer is seen in the distance from which the "little brown men" are debouching in quantity. In the foreground of the picture are to be seen the "bats" used by the whites, while the knotty club of "False-Personation" indicates another of the means by which the Restriction Act is "knocked out of time." Altogether the lesson of the hour is graphically set forth in this telling picture. [*The Wasp*, 15 August 1885, p. 3.]

EPILOGUE: THE REPEAL

The 1882 Chinese Exclusion Act and its extensions set a precedent by which the United States government could ban an entire ethnic group from entering the country, as well as deny them naturalization rights. This culminated in the Immigration Act of 1924, also known as the Asian Exclusion Act, which excluded all aliens ineligible to citizenship from immigration. The 1790 Naturalization Act allowed only "free white persons" to become American citizens. Following the aftermath of the Civil War, the Emancipation Proclamation of 1863 granted people of African descent the privilege of naturalization. Ten years later, the Naturalization Act was amended with specific language to include persons of African descent so as not to include the Chinese. In other words, only Asians as a group of people were ineligible to American citizenship and hence could not immigrate under the 1924 Act.

When the United States declared war against Japan on December 8, 1941, almost overnight China became an ally. The Chinese were portrayed as heroic people united with Americans in the struggle against a common enemy. However, this newfound alliance was severely strained by the existence of the Chinese Exclusion Acts. Japanese war propaganda used these acts as examples of undemocratic and racist behavior on the part of the United States. Bound by treaties and alliance, the Chinese began to question America's sincerity when it was obvious that the Chinese in America were not treated equally. Japan had effectively used Chinese exclusion to weaken the ties between China and America.

The Exclusion Acts had been effective in reducing the Chinese population, especially in California. By 1940, they were only one half of one percent of the state's population. Unemployment was no longer an issue in a wartime boom economy. The Chinese were consequently not seen as a threat and China was now considered a potentially lucrative market. By the turn of the century, the Chinese Yellow Peril was basically arrested and America focused more on the Japanese Yellow Peril.

Beginning in February 1943, many House resolutions were introduced to repeal the Chinese Exclusion Acts. On February 17, 1943, Martin J. Kennedy (New York) introduced the first of a series of House resolutions, ironically numbered H.R. 1882, that would repeal the Chinese Exclusion Acts and give the Chinese the right to naturalization. The final version was submitted by Warren G. Magnuson (Washington) as H.R. 3070. The House debated and passed the Magnuson Bill in October 21; the Senate followed suit in November 26. On December 17, 1943, President Franklin D. Roosevelt signed the bill into law, ending sixty-one years of exclusion. A token annual immigration quota was set at 105. More importantly, the Chinese were now eligible to become United States citizens.

It is worthy to take note of the significance of the Chinese

Exclusion Act in its sixty-one years of existence and subsequent repeal. First, while the United States participated in the effort to "open up" China for European and American trade and missionary activities, it simultaneously demanded a "closed door" policy at home, shutting out Chinese immigration. The "open door" philosophy of the 19th century was the United States' attempt to obtain an equal opportunity to exploit China's perceived wealth. Second, by the mid-1860s, the United States had already experienced several years of civil war in the alleged effort to abolish slavery. Fifteen years after the war, the federal government adopted the Chinese Exclusion Act. Thus, while Civil War rhetoric represented "a great leap forward" towards racial equality in America, the Chinese Exclusion Act signified "a great fall backwards." Third, the act had an international impact as it became a model for similar laws in other countries like Canada and Mexico. Fourth, this federally sanctioned action set a precedent for future racist policies against other ethnic minority groups, as highlighted in the case of the Japanese Americans during World War II. While the Chinese Exclusion Acts were repealed in 1943, nearly 120,000 Japanese, both alien and United States citizens, had already been put into concentration camps under Presidential Executive Order 9066, violating their citizenship and constitutional rights. Lastly, the Repeal Act granted the Chinese the right to naturalize and become citizens, but other Asians were denied these same rights. It appeared that America's attempt to correct its own racist policies was highly selective, extending only to allies, and even then with severe limitations. It should be pointed out that the repeal allowed a grand total of 105 Chinese per year to immigrate to the United States.

Without a doubt, Chinese exclusion has left a legacy of racism. The civil rights movement of the early 1960s helped to bring about an equitable immigration policy in 1965, when for the first time Asian countries were given quotas comparable to that of European countries. However, in terms of domestic politics, hate crimes against Asians still exist, testifying to the continued scapegoating of Asians in America during times of economic decline and unemployment. This phenomenon is no different from that of the West Coast during the 1870s. Current anti-Asian violence, rhetoric, and a renewed call for restrictive immigration policies sound frighteningly familiar to those who know American history. "The Coming Man" was indeed a prophecy of our country's continuing racial relations towards all Asians.

1990   The United States passed a new immigration bill to modify the 1965 Immigration Act. The quota for immigrants with special skills was increased. Originally, the sponsors of the bill intended to abolish the immigration rights of alien siblings; this was reinstated after numerous protests from Asian and Latino lobby groups.

U.S. Census figures show Asian/Pacific Islanders comprising less than 3% of the total U.S. population.

POPULATION OF CHINESE IN THE UNITED STATES (1860-1990)
(Based on U.S. Census Figures)

YEAR	TOTAL U.S. POPULATION	TOTAL CHINESE POPULATION
1860	31,443,321	34,933
1870	38,558,371	63,199
1880	50,155,783	105,465
1890	62,947,714	107,488
1900*	76,212,168	118,746
1910	92,228,531	94,414
1920	106,021,568	85,202
1930	123,202,660	102,159
1940	132,165,129	106,334
1950	151,325,798	150,005
1960	179,323,732	237,292
1970	203,211,926	436,062
1980	226,545,805	812,178
1990	248,709,873	1,645,472

*Includes Hawaii and Alaska. Figures excluding Hawaii and Alaska for 1900 would be 75,994,575 and 89,863 respectively.

APPENDIX III: Selected Bibliography

English Language Works

Arkush, R. David and Lee, Leo O., ed. *Land Without Ghosts, Chinese Impressions of America from the Mid-Nineteenth Century to the Present.* Berkeley, Los Angeles, and London: University of California Press, 1989.

Baldwin, S.L. *Must Chinese Go? An Examination of the Chinese Question.* New York: Press of H.B. Elkins, 1890.

Becker, Jules. *The Course of Exclusion, 1882-1924 San Francisco Newspaper Coverage of the Chinese and Japanese in the United States.* Lewiston, NY: The Edwin Mellen Press, 1991.

Chan, Sucheng, ed. *Entry Denied, Exclusion and the Chinese Community in America, 1882-1943.* Philadelphia: Temple University Press, 1991.

Char, Tin Yuke, ed. *The Sandalwood Mountains: Readings and Stories of the Early Chinese in Hawaii.* Honolulu: University Press of Hawaii, 1975.

Coolidge, Mary Elizabeth. *Chinese Immigration.* New York: Henry Holt and Company, 1909.

Cross, Ira B. *A History of the Labor Movement in California.* Berkeley: University of California Press, 1935.

Davis, Winfield J. *History of Political Conventions in California, 1849-1892.* Sacramento: California State Library, 1893.

Dooner, P.W. *Last Days of the Republic.* San Francisco: Alta California Publishing House, 1880.

Foner, Philip S. *History of the Labor Movement in the United States, From Colonial Times to the Founding of the American Federation of Labor.* Vol. 1. New York: International Publishers Co., Inc., 1975.

Hom, Marlon K. *Songs of Gold Mountain, Cantonese Rhymes from San Francisco Chinatown.* Berkeley, Los Angeles, and Oxford: University of California Press, 1987.

Johnson, Kenneth M. *The Sting of the Wasp, Political and Satirical Cartoons from the Truculent Early San Francisco Weekly.* San Francisco: The Book Club of California, 1967.

LaFargue, Thomas E. *China's First Hundred, Educational Mission Students in the United States 1872-1881.* Pullman, WA: Washington State University Press, 1987.

Lai, Him Mark. *A History Reclaimed, An Annotated Bibliography of Chinese Language Materials on the Chinese of America.* Los Angeles: Asian American Studies Center, University of California, 1986.

—— and Choy, Philip P. *Outlines, History of the Chinese in America.* San Francisco: Chinese-American Studies Planning Group, 1971.

——, Lim, Genny, and Yung, Judy. *Island, Poetry and History of Chinese Immigrants on Angel Island 1910-1940.* San Francisco: HOC DOI (History of Chinese Detained on Island), 1980.

Li Tien-Lu. *Congressional Policy of Chinese Immigration, or Legislation Relating to Chinese Immigration to the United States.* Nashville, TN: Publishing House of the Methodist Episcopal Church, South, 1916.

Lo, Karl and Lai, Him Mark, comps. *Chinese Newspapers Published in North America, 1854-1975.* Washington, D.C.: Center for Chinese Research Materials, 1977.

Low, Victor. *The Unimpressible Race, A Century of Educational Struggle by the Chinese in San Francisco.* San Francisco: East/West Publishing Company, Inc., 1982.

McCunn, Ruthanne Lum. *Chinese American Portraits, Personal Histories 1828-1988.* San Francisco: Chronicle Books, 1988.

McClain, Charles J. *In Search of Equality, The Chinese Struggle Against Discrimination in Nineteenth-Century America.* Berkeley, Los Angeles, and London: University of California Press, 1994.

McKee, Delber L. *Chinese Exclusion Versus the Open Door Policy, 1900-1906, Clashes over China Policy in the Roosevelt Era.* Detroit, MI: Wayne State University Press, 1977.

Mears, Eliot Grinnell. *Resident Orientals on the American Pacific Coast: Their Legal and Economic Status.* Chicago: University of Chicago Press, 1928.

Miller, Stuart Creighton. *The Unwelcome Immigrant, The American Image of the Chinese, 1785-1882.* Berkeley, Los Angeles, and London: University of California Press, 1969.

Mott, Frank Luther. *A History of American Magazines.* 5 vols. Cambridge, MA: The Belknap Press of Harvard University Press, 1938-1968.

Riggs, Fred W. *Pressures on Congress, A Study of the Repeal of Chinese Exclusion.* New York: King's Crown Press, 1950.

Sandmeyer, Elmer C. *The Anti-Chinese Movement in California.* Urbana, IL: University of Illinois Press, 1939.

Saxton, Alexander. *The Indispensable Enemy, Labor and the Anti-Chinese Movement in California.* Berkeley, Los Angeles, and London: University of California Press, 1971.

Seward, George F. *Chinese Immigration in Its Social and Economical Aspects.* New York: Scribners, 1881.

Sung, Betty Lee. *Mountain of Gold, The Story of the Chinese in America.* New York: Macmillan, 1967.

Tsai, Shih-shan Henry. *China and the Overseas Chinese in the United States, 1868-1911.* Fayetteville, AK: University of Arkansas Pres, 1983.

Wu, Cheng-tsu, ed. *"Chink!" A Documentary History of Anti-Chinese Prejudice in America.* New York: The World Publishing Co., 1972.

Wu, William. *The Yellow Peril, Chinese Americans in American Fiction, 1850-1940.* Hamden, CT: Archon Books, 1982.

Yung, Judy. *Chinese Women of America, A Pictorial History.* Seattle and London: University of Washington Press, 1986.

Chinese Language Works

吳尚鷹著：《美國華僑百年紀實》，香港：一九五四年版

劉伯驥著：《美國華僑史》，台北：黎明文化事業公司，一九七六年版

劉伯驥著：《美國華僑史續編》，台北：黎明文化事公司，一九八一年版

劉伯驥著：《美國華僑逸史》，台北：黎明文化事業公司，一九八四年版

呂浦　張振鵾合著：《黃禍論：歷史資料選輯》。北京：中國科學出版社，一九七九年版

陳翰笙主編：《華工出國史料》第三輯（美國外交和國會文件選譯），北京：中華書局，
　　一九八一年版

楊國標　劉漢標　楊安堯合著：《美國華僑史》，廣州：廣東高等教育出版社，一九八九年版

麥禮謙著：《從華僑到華人──二十世紀美國華人社會發展史》，香港：三聯書店，一九九二年版

李定一：《中美早期外交史──1784～1894年》台北：三民書局，一九七八年初版，
　　一九八五年再版

阿英編：《反美華工禁約文學集》，北京：中華書局，一九六二年版

APPENDIX IV:　English-Chinese Glossary

Burlingame Treaty, 1868	蒲安臣條約（即天津條約）
Chen, Lanbin	陳蘭彬
Cheng, Edward Tak-Wah	鄭德華
Chinese American Citizens' Alliance	同源會
Chinese Consolidated Benevolent Association	中華會館
Chinese Historical Society of America	美國華人歷史學會
Choy, Philip P.	胡垣坤
Choy, Randall	胡紹章
Choy, Sarah	黃念慈
Chung, Chuong H.	鍾章宏
"Confession Program"	坦白措施
Cui, Guoyin [Tsui Kuo-yin]	崔國因
Dong, Lorraine	曾露凌
Fong, Hiram	鄺友良
Fung, Robert	馮灼倫
Hom, Marlon K.	譚雅倫
Lai, Him Mark	麥禮謙
Luk, Judith	陸詠笑
muk-uk	木屋
Ouyang, Ming	歐陽明
"paper son"	冒藉，假紙
Wang-Hea Treaty [*Wang-Hia Treaty*], 1848	望廈條約
Wu, Tingfang	伍廷芳
Yang, Ru	楊儒
Yung, Judy	楊碧芳
Yung, Wing	容閎
Zheng, Zaoru	鄭藻如

SPSS
Regression Models™ *10.0*

Marija J. Norušis/ SPSS Inc.

For more information about SPSS® software products, please visit our WWW site at *http://www.spss.com* or contact

Marketing Department
SPSS Inc.
233 South Wacker Drive, 11th Floor
Chicago, IL 60606-6307
Tel: (312) 651-3000
Fax: (312) 651-3668

Preface

SPSS® 10.0 is a powerful software package for microcomputer data management and analysis. The Regression Models option is an add-on enhancement that provides additional statistical analysis techniques. The procedures in Regression Models must be used with the SPSS 10.0 Base and are completely integrated into that system.

The Regression Models option includes procedures for:
- Weighted and two-stage least-squares regression
- Logistic regression
- Multinomial regression
- Nonlinear regression

Installation

To install Regression Models, follow the instructions for adding and removing features in the installation instructions supplied with the SPSS Base. (To start, double-click on the SPSS Setup icon.)

Compatibility

The SPSS system is designed to operate on many computer systems. See the materials that came with your system for specific information on minimum and recommended requirements.

Serial Numbers

Your serial number is your identification number with SPSS Inc. You will need this serial number when you call SPSS Inc. for information regarding support, payment, or an upgraded system. The serial number was provided with your Base system. Before using the system, please copy this number to the registration card.

Registration Card

Don't put it off: *fill out and send us your registration card.* Until we receive your registration card, you have an unregistered system. Even if you have previously sent a card to us, please fill out and return the card enclosed in your Regression Models package. Registering your system entitles you to:

- Technical support services
- New product announcements and upgrade announcements

Customer Service

If you have any questions concerning your shipment or account, contact your local office, listed on page vi. Please have your serial number ready for identification when calling.

Training Seminars

SPSS Inc. provides both public and onsite training seminars for SPSS. All seminars feature hands-on workshops. SPSS seminars will be offered in major U.S. and European cities on a regular basis. For more information on these seminars, call your local office, listed on page vi.

Technical Support

The services of SPSS Technical Support are available to registered customers. Customers may call Technical Support for assistance in using SPSS products or for installation help for one of the supported hardware environments. To reach Technical Support, see the SPSS home page on the World Wide Web at *http://www.spss.com*, or call your local office, listed on page vi. Be prepared to identify yourself, your organization, and the serial number of your system.

Additional Publications

Additional copies of SPSS product manuals may be purchased from Prentice Hall, the exclusive distributor of SPSS publications. To order, fill out and mail the Publications order form included with your system or call toll-free. If you represent a bookstore or have an account with Prentice Hall, call 1-800-223-1360. If you are not an account customer, call 1-800-374-1200. In Canada, call 1-800-567-3800. Outside of North America, contact your local Prentice Hall office.

Except for academic course adoptions, manuals can also be purchased from SPSS Inc. Contact your local SPSS office, listed on page vi.

Tell Us Your Thoughts

Your comments are important. Please send us a letter and let us know about your experiences with SPSS products. We especially like to hear about new and interesting applications using the SPSS system. Write to SPSS Inc. Marketing Department, Attn: Director of Product Planning, 233 South Wacker Drive, 11th Floor, Chicago, IL 60606-6307.

About This Manual

This manual documents the graphical user interface for the statistical procedures included in the Regression Models module. Illustrations of dialog boxes are taken from SPSS for Windows. Dialog boxes in other operating systems are similar. In addition, this manual provides examples of statistical procedures and advice on interpreting the output. The Regression Models command syntax, formerly included in this manual, is now available in the *SPSS Syntax Reference Guide Release 10.0.* It is also available online with the CD-ROM version of SPSS.

Contacting SPSS

If you would like to be on our mailing list, contact one of our offices, listed on page vi, or visit our WWW site at *http://www.spss.com.* We will send you a copy of our newsletter and let you know about SPSS Inc. activities in your area.

SPSS Inc.
Chicago, Illinois, U.S.A.
Tel: 1.312.651.3000
www.spss.com/corpinfo
Customer Service:
1.800.521.1337
Sales:
1.800.543.2185
sales@spss.com
Training:
1.800.543.6607
Technical Support:
1.312.651.3410
support@spss.com

SPSS Federal Systems
Tel: 1.703.527.6777
www.spss.com

SPSS Argentina srl
Tel: +5411.4814.5030
www.spss.com

SPSS Asia Pacific Pte. Ltd.
Tel: +65.245.9110
www.spss.com

SPSS Australasia Pty. Ltd.
Tel: +61.2.9954.5660
www.spss.com

SPSS Belgium
Tel: +32.162.389.82
www.spss.com

SPSS Benelux BV
Tel: +31.183.651777
www.spss.nl

SPSS Brasil Ltda
Tel: +55.11.5505.3644
www.spss.com

SPSS Czech Republic
Tel: +420.2.24813839
www.spss.cz

SPSS Danmark A/S
Tel: +45.45.46.02.00
www.spss.com

SPSS Finland Oy
Tel: +358.9.524.801
www.spss.com

SPSS France SARL
Tel: +01.55.35.27.00 x03
www.spss.com

SPSS Germany
Tel: +49.89.4890740
www.spss.com

SPSS Hellas SA
Tel: +30.1.72.51.925/72.51.950
www.spss.com

SPSS Hispanoportuguesa S.L.
Tel: +34.91.447.37.00
www.spss.com

SPSS Hong Kong Ltd.
Tel: +852.2.811.9662
www.spss.com

SPSS India
Tel: +91.80.225.0260
www.spss.com

SPSS Ireland
Tel: +353.1.496.9007
www.spss.com

SPSS Israel Ltd.
Tel: +972.9.9526700
www.spss.com

SPSS Italia srl
Tel: +39.51.252573
www.spss.it

SPSS Japan Inc.
Tel: +81.3.5466.5511
www.spss.com

SPSS Kenya Limited
Tel: +254.2.577.262/3
www.spss.com

SPSS Korea KIC Co., Ltd.
Tel: +82.2.3446.7651
www.spss.co.kr

SPSS Latin America
Tel: +1.312.651.3539
www.spss.com

SPSS Malaysia Sdn Bhd
Tel: +60.3.7873.6477
www.spss.com

SPSS Mexico SA de CV
Tel: +52.5.682.87.68
www.spss.com

SPSS Norway
Tel: +47.22.40.20.60
www.spss.com

SPSS Polska
Tel: +48.12.6369680
www.companion.krakow.pl

SPSS Russia
Tel: +7.095.125.0069
www.spss.com

SPSS Sweden AB
Tel: +46.8.506.105.68
www.spss.com

SPSS Schweiz AG
Tel: +41.1.266.90.30
www.spss.com

SPSS BI (Singapore) Pte. Ltd.
Tel: +65.324.5150
www.spss.com

SPSS South Africa
Tel: +27.11.807.3189
www.spss.com

SPSS Taiwan Corp.
Taipei, Republic of China
Tel: +886.2.25771100
www.spss.com

SPSS (Thailand) Co., Ltd.
Tel: +66.2.260.7070, +66.2.260.7080
www.spss.com

SPSS UK Ltd.
Tel: +44.1483.719200
www.spss.com

Contents

Choosing a Procedure for Binary Logistic Regression Models

Binary logistic regression models can be fitted using either the Logistic Regression procedure or the Multinomial Logistic Regression procedure. Each procedure has options not available in the other. An important theoretical distinction is that the Logistic Regression procedure produces all predictions, residuals, influence statistics, and goodness-of-fit tests using data at the individual case level, regardless of how the data are entered and whether or not the number of covariate patterns is smaller than the total number of cases, while the Multinomial Logistic Regression procedure internally aggregates cases to form subpopulations with identical covariate patterns for the predictors, producing predictions, residuals, and goodness-of-fit tests based on these subpopulations. If all predictors are categorical or any continuous predictors take on only a limited number of values—so that there are several cases at each distinct covariate pattern—the subpopulation approach can produce valid goodness of fit tests and informative residuals, while the individual case level approach cannot.

Logistic Regression provides the following unique features:

- Hosmer-Lemeshow test of goodness of fit for the model
- Stepwise analyses
- Contrasts to define model parameterization
- Alternative cut points for classification
- Classification plots
- Model fitted on one set of cases to a held-out set of cases
- Saves predictions, residuals, and influence statistics

Multinomial Logistic Regression provides the following unique features:

- Pearson and deviance chi-square tests for goodness of fit of the model
- Specification of subpopulations for grouping of data for goodness-of-fit tests
- Listing of counts, predicted counts, and residuals by subpopulations
- Correction of variance estimates for over-dispersion
- Covariance matrix of the parameter estimates

- Tests of linear combinations of parameters
- Explicit specification of nested models
- Fit 1-1 matched conditional logistic regression models using differenced variables

2 Logistic Regression

Logistic regression is useful for situations in which you want to be able to predict the presence or absence of a characteristic or outcome based on values of a set of predictor variables. It is similar to a linear regression model but is suited to models where the dependent variable is dichotomous. Logistic regression coefficients can be used to estimate odds ratios for each of the independent variables in the model. Logistic regression is applicable to a broader range of research situations than discriminant analysis.

Example. What lifestyle characteristics are risk factors for coronary heart disease (CHD)? Given a sample of patients measured on smoking status, diet, exercise, alcohol use, and CHD status, you could build a model using the four lifestyle variables to predict the presence or absence of CHD in a sample of patients. The model can then be used to derive estimates of the odds ratios for each factor to tell you, for example, how much more likely smokers are to develop CHD than nonsmokers.

Statistics. For each analysis: total cases, selected cases, valid cases. For each categorical variable: parameter coding. For each step: variable(s) entered or removed, iteration history, −2 log-likelihood, goodness of fit, Hosmer-Lemeshow goodness-of-fit statistic, model chi-square, improvement chi-square, classification table, correlations between variables, observed groups and predicted probabilities chart, residual chi-square. For each variable in the equation: coefficient (B), standard error of B, Wald statistic, R, estimated odds ratio ($\exp(B)$), confidence interval for $\exp(B)$, log-likelihood if term removed from model. For each variable not in the equation: score statistic, R. For each case: observed group, predicted probability, predicted group, residual, standardized residual.

Methods. You can estimate models using block entry of variables or any of the following stepwise methods: forward conditional, forward LR, forward Wald, backward conditional, backward LR, or backward Wald.

Data. The dependent variable should be dichotomous. Independent variables can be interval level or categorical; if categorical, they should be dummy or indicator coded (there is an option in the procedure to recode categorical variables automatically).

Assumptions. Logistic regression does not rely on distributional assumptions in the same sense that discriminant analysis does. However, your solution may be more stable if your predictors have a multivariate normal distribution. Additionally, as with other forms of regression, multicollinearity among the predictors can lead to biased estimates and inflated standard errors. The procedure is most effective when group membership is

3

a truly categorical variable; if group membership is based on values of a continuous variable (for example, "high IQ" versus "low IQ"), you should consider using linear regression to take advantage of the richer information offered by the continuous variable itself.

Related procedures. Use the Scatterplot procedure to screen your data for multicollinearity. If assumptions of multivariate normality and equal variance-covariance matrices are met, you may be able to get a quicker solution using the Discriminant Analysis procedure. If all of your predictor variables are categorical, you can also use the Loglinear procedure. If your dependent variable is continuous, use the Linear Regression procedure.

To Obtain a Logistic Regression Analysis

▶ From the menus choose:

Analyze
  Regression
    Binary Logistic…

Figure 2.1   Expanded Logistic Regression dialog box

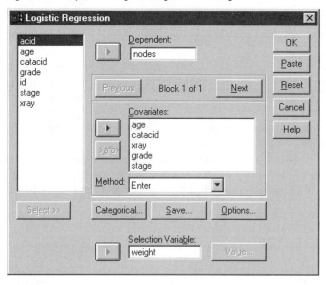

▶ Select one dichotomous dependent variable. This variable may be numeric or short string.

▶ Select one or more covariates. To include interaction terms, select all of the variables involved in the interaction and then select >a*b>.

▶ To enter variables in groups (blocks), select the covariates for a block, and click *Next* to specify a new block. Repeat until all blocks have been specified.

Optionally, you can select cases for analysis. Click *Select*, choose a selection variable, and click *Rule*.

Logistic Regression Set Rule

Figure 2.2   Logistic Regression Set Rule dialog box

Cases defined by the selection rule are included in the model estimation. For example, if you selected a variable and *equals* and specified a value of 5, then only the cases for which the selected variable has a value equal to 5 are included in the model estimation.

Statistics and classification results are generated for both selected and unselected cases. This provides a mechanism for classifying new cases based on previously existing data, or for partitioning your data into training and testing subsets, to perform validation on the model generated.

Logistic Regression Define Categorical Variables

Figure 2.3   Logistic Regression Define Categorical Variables dialog box

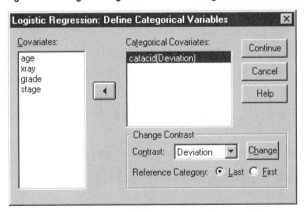

You can specify details of how the Logistic Regression procedure will handle categorical variables:

Covariates. Contains a list of all of the covariates specified in the main dialog box, either by themselves or as part of an interaction, in any layer. If some of these are string variables or are categorical, you can use them only as categorical covariates.

Categorical Covariates. Lists variables identified as categorical. Each variable includes a notation in parentheses indicating the contrast coding to be used. String variables (denoted by the symbol < following their names) are already present in the Categorical Covariates list. Select any other categorical covariates from the Covariates list and move them into the Categorical Covariates list.

Change Contrast. Allows you to change the contrast method. Available contrast methods are:

- **Deviation.** Each category of the predictor variable except the reference category is compared to the overall effect.

- **Simple.** Each category of the predictor variable (except the reference category) is compared to the reference category.

- **Difference.** Each category of the predictor variable except the first category is compared to the average effect of previous categories. Also known as reverse Helmert contrasts.

- **Helmert.** Each category of the predictor variable except the last category is compared to the average effect of subsequent categories.

- **Repeated.** Each category of the predictor variable except the first category is compared to the category that precedes it.

- **Polynomial.** Orthogonal polynomial contrasts. Categories are assumed to be equally spaced. Polynomial contrasts are available for numeric variables only.

- **Indicator.** Contrasts indicate the presence or absence of category membership. The reference category is represented in the contrast matrix as a row of zeros.

If you select *Deviation*, *Simple*, or *Indicator*, select either *First* or *Last* as the reference category. Note that the method is not actually changed until you click *Change*.

String covariates *must* be categorical covariates. To remove a string variable from the Categorical Covariates list, you must remove all terms containing the variable from the Covariates list in the main dialog box.

Logistic Regression Save New Variables

Figure 2.4   Logistic Regression Save New Variables dialog box

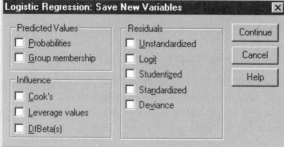

You can save results of the logistic regression as new variables in the working data file:

Predicted Values. Saves values predicted by the model. Available options are Probabilities and Group membership.

Influence. Saves values from statistics that measure the influence of cases on predicted values. Available options are Cook's, Leverage values, and DfBeta(s).

Residuals. Saves residuals. Available options are Unstandardized, Logit, Studentized, Standardized, and Deviance.

Logistic Regression Options

Figure 2.5   Logistic Regression Options dialog box

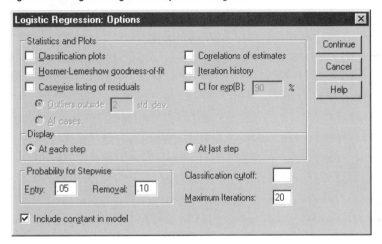

You can specify options for your logistic regression analysis:

Statistics and Plots. Allows you to request statistics and plots. Available options are Classification plots, Hosmer-Lemeshow goodness-of-fit, Casewise listing of residuals, Correlations of estimates, Iteration history, and CI for exp(B). Select one of the alternatives in the Display group to display statistics and plots either At each step or, only for the final model, At last step.

Probability for Stepwise. Allows you to control the criteria by which variables are entered into and removed from the equation. You can specify criteria for entry or removal of variables.

Classification cutoff. Allows you to determine the cut point for classifying cases. Cases with predicted values that exceed the classification cutoff are classified as positive, while those with predicted values smaller than the cutoff are classified as negative. To change the default, enter a value between 0.01 and 0.99.

Maximum Iterations. Allows you to change the maximum number of times that the model iterates before terminating.

Include constant in model. Allows you to indicate whether the model should include a constant term. If disabled, the constant term will equal 0.

LOGISTIC REGRESSION Command Additional Features

The SPSS command language also allows you to:

- Identify casewise output by the values or variable labels of a variable.
- Control the spacing of iteration reports. Rather than printing parameter estimates after every iteration, you can request parameter estimates after every nth iteration.
- Change the criteria for terminating iteration and checking for redundancy.
- Specify a variable list for casewise listings.
- Conserve memory by holding the data for each split-file group in an external scratch file during processing.

3 Multinomial Logistic Regression

Multinomial Logistic Regression is useful for situations in which you want to be able to classify subjects based on values of a set of predictor variables. This type of regression is similar to logistic regression, but it is more general because the dependent variable is not restricted to two categories.

Example. In order to market films more effectively, movie studios want to predict what type of film a moviegoer is likely to see. By performing a Multinomial Logistic Regression, the studio can determine the strength of influence a person's age, gender, and dating status has upon the type of film they prefer. The studio can then slant the advertising campaign of a particular movie towards a group of people likely to go see it.

Statistics. Iteration history, parameter coefficients, asymptotic covariance and correlation matrices, likelihood-ratio tests for model and partial effects, –2 log-likelihood. Pearson and deviance chi-square goodness of fit. Cox and Snell, Nagelkerke, and McFadden R^2. Classification: observed versus predicted frequencies by response category. Crosstabulation: observed and predicted frequencies (with residuals) and proportions by covariate pattern and response category.

Methods. A multinomial logit model is fit for the full factorial model, or a user-specified model. Parameter estimation is performed through an iterative maximum-likelihood algorithm.

Data. The dependent variable should be categorical. Independent variables can be factors or covariates. In general, factors should be categorical variables and covariates should be continuous variables.

Assumptions. It is assumed that the odds ratio of any two categories are independent of all other response categories. For example, if a new product is introduced to a market, this assumption states that the market shares of all other products are affected proportionally equally. Also, given a covariate pattern, the responses are assumed to be independent multinomial variables.

To Obtain a Multinomial Logistic Regression

▶ From the menus choose:

Analyze
  Regression
    Multinomial Logistic…

Figure 3.1   Multinomial Logistic Regression dialog box

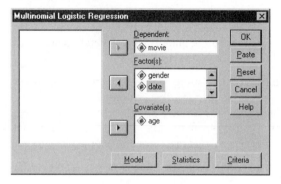

▶ Select one dependent variable.

▶ Factors are optional and can be either numeric or categorical.

▶ Covariates are optional but must be numeric if specified.

Multinomial Logistic Regression Models

Figure 3.2   Multinomial Logistic Regression Model dialog box

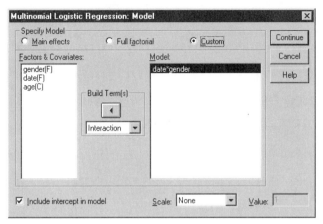

You can specify the following models for your Multinomial Logistic Regression:

Specify Model. A main-effects model contains the covariate and factor main effects but no interaction effects. A full factorial model contains all main effects and all factor-by-factor interactions. It does not contain covariate interactions. You can create a custom model to specify subsets of factor interactions or covariate interactions.

Factors and Covariates. The factors and covariates are listed with (F) for factor and (C) for covariate.

Model. The model depends on the main and interaction effects you select.

Include intercept in model. Allows you to include or exclude an intercept term for the model.

Scale. Allows you to specify the dispersion scaling value that will be used to correct the estimate of the parameter covariance matrix. Deviance estimates the scaling value using the deviance function (likelihood-ratio chi-square) statistic. Pearson estimates the scaling value using the Pearson chi-square statistic. You can also specify your own scaling value. It must be a positive numeric value.

Build Terms

For the selected factors and covariates:

Main effects. Creates a main-effects term for each variable selected.

Interaction. Creates the highest-level interaction term of all selected variables.

All 2-way. Creates all possible two-way interactions of the selected variables.

All 3-way. Creates all possible three-way interactions of the selected variables.

All 4-way. Creates all possible four-way interactions of the selected variables.

All 5-way. Creates all possible five-way interactions of the selected variables.

Multinomial Logistic Regression Statistics

Figure 3.3   Multinomial Logistic Regression Statistics dialog box

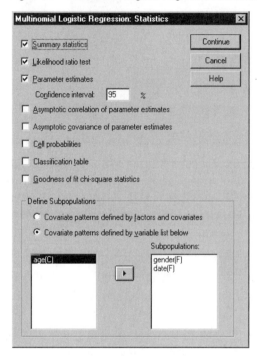

You can specify the following statistics for your Multinomial Logistic Regression:

Summary statistics. Prints the Cox and Snell, Nagelkerke, and McFadden R^2 statistics.

Likelihood ratio test. Prints likelihood-ratio tests for the model partial effects. The test for the overall model is printed automatically.

Parameter estimates. Prints estimates of the model effects, with a user-specified level of confidence.

Asymptotic correlation of parameter estimates. Prints matrix of parameter estimate correlations.

Asymptotic covariance of parameter estimates. Prints matrix of parameter estimate covariances.

Cell probabilities. Prints a table of the observed and expected frequencies (with residual) and proportions by covariate pattern and response category.

Classification table. Prints a table of the observed versus predicted responses.

Goodness of fit chi-square statistics. Prints Pearson and likelihood-ratio chi-square statistics. Statistics are computed for the covariate patterns determined by all factors and covariates or by a user-defined subset of the factors and covariates.

Define Subpopulations. Allows you to select a subset of the factors and covariates in order to define the covariate patterns used by cell probabilities and the goodness-of-fit tests.

Multinomial Logistic Regression Convergence Criteria

Figure 3.4   Multinomial Logistic Regression Convergence Criteria dialog box

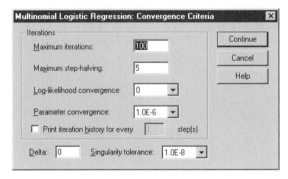

You can specify the following criteria for your Multinomial Logistic Regression:

Iterations. Allows you to specify the maximum number of times you want to cycle through the algorithm, the maximum number of steps in the step-halving, the convergence tolerances for changes in the log-likelihood and parameters, and how often the progress of the iterative algorithm is printed.

Delta. Allows you to specify a non-negative value less than 1. This value is added to each cell in the crosstabulation of response category by covariate pattern. This is useful when some cells have zero observations.

Singularity tolerance. Allows you to specify the tolerance used in checking for singularities.

Multinomial Logistic Regression Save

Figure 3.5   Multinomial Logistic Regression Save dialog box

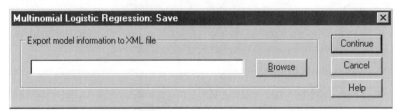

The Save dialog box allows you to export model information to the specified file. *Smart-Score* and future releases of *WhatIf?* will be able to use this file.

NOMREG Command Additional Features

The SPSS command language also allows you to:

- Include cases with user-missing values.
- Customize hypothesis tests by specifying null hypotheses as linear combinations of parameters.

4 Probit Analysis

This procedure measures the relationship between the strength of a stimulus and the proportion of cases exhibiting a certain response to the stimulus. It is useful for situations where you have a dichotomous output that is thought to be influenced or caused by levels of some independent variable(s) and is particularly well suited to experimental data. This procedure will allow you to estimate the strength of a stimulus required to induce a certain proportion of responses, such as the median effective dose.

This procedure uses the algorithms proposed and implemented in NPSOL ® by Gill, Murray, Saunders & Wright to estimate the model parameters.

Example. How effective is a new pesticide at killing ants, and what is an appropriate concentration to use? You might perform an experiment in which you expose samples of ants to different concentrations of the pesticide and then record the number of ants killed and the number of ants exposed. Applying probit analysis to these data, you can determine the strength of the relationship between concentration and killing, and you can determine what the appropriate concentration of pesticide would be if you wanted to be sure to kill, say, 95% of exposed ants.

Statistics. Regression coefficients and standard errors, intercept and standard error, Pearson goodness-of-fit chi-square, observed and expected frequencies, and confidence intervals for effective levels of independent variable(s). Plots: transformed response plots.

Data. For each value of the independent variable (or each combination of values for multiple independent variables), your response variable should be a count of the number of cases with those values that show the response of interest, and the total observed variable should be a count of the total number of cases with those values for the independent variable. The factor variable should be categorical, coded as integers.

Assumptions. Observations should be independent. If you have a large number of values for the independent variables relative to the number of observations, as you might in an observational study, the chi-square and goodness-of-fit statistics may not be valid.

Related procedures. Probit analysis is closely related to logistic regression; in fact, if you choose the logit transformation, this procedure will essentially compute a logistic regression. In general, probit analysis is appropriate for designed experiments, whereas logistic regression is more appropriate for observational studies. The differences in output reflect these different emphases. The probit analysis procedure reports estimates of effective values for various rates of response (including median effective dose), while the logistic regression procedure reports estimates of odds ratios for independent variables.

To Obtain a Probit Analysis

▶ From the menus choose:

Analyze
  Regression
    Probit...

Figure 4.1   Probit Analysis dialog box

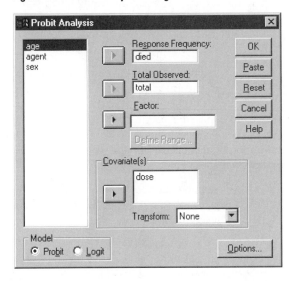

▶ Select a response frequency variable. This variable indicates the number of cases exhibiting a response to the test stimulus. The values of this variable cannot be negative.

▶ Select a total observed variable. This variable indicates the number of cases to which the stimulus was applied. The values of this variable cannot be negative and cannot be less than the values of the response frequency variable for each case.

Optionally, you can select a factor variable. If you do, click *Define Range* to define the groups.

▶ Select one or more covariate(s). This variable contains the level of the stimulus applied to each observation. If you want to transform the covariate, select a transformation from the Transform drop-down list. If no transformation is applied, and there is a control group, then the control group is included in the analysis.

▶ Select either *Probit* or *Logit* model.

Probit Analysis Define Range

Figure 4.2   Probit Analysis Define Range dialog box

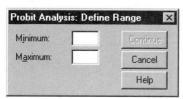

This allows you to specify the levels of the factor variable that will be analyzed. The factor levels must be coded as consecutive integers, and all levels in the range you specify will be analyzed.

Probit Analysis Options

Figure 4.3   Probit Analysis Options dialog box

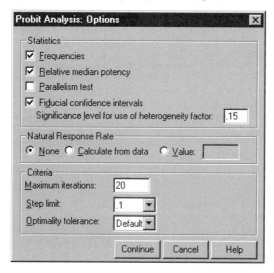

You can specify options for your probit analysis:

Statistics. Allows you to request the following optional statistics: Frequencies, Relative median potency, Parallelism test, and Fiducial confidence intervals.

Fiducial confidence intervals and Relative median potency are unavailable if you have selected more than one covariate. Relative median potency and Parallelism test are available only if you have selected a factor variable.

Natural Response Rate. Allows you to indicate a natural response rate even in the absence of the stimulus. Available alternatives are None, Calculate from data, or Value.

Criteria. Allows you to control parameters of the iterative parameter-estimation algorithm. You can override the defaults for maximum iterations, step limit, and optimality tolerance.

PROBIT Command Additional Features

The SPSS command language also allows you to:

- Request an analysis on both the probit and logit models.
- Control the treatment of missing values.
- Transform the covariates by bases other than base 10 or natural log.

5 Nonlinear Regression

Nonlinear regression is a method of finding a nonlinear model of the relationship between the dependent variable and a set of independent variables. Unlike traditional linear regression, which is restricted to estimating linear models, nonlinear regression can estimate models with arbitrary relationships between independent and dependent variables. This is accomplished using iterative estimation algorithms. Note that this procedure is not necessary for simple polynomial models of the form $Y = A + BX**2$. By defining $W = X**2$, we get a simple linear model, $Y = A + BW$, which can be estimated using traditional methods such as the Linear Regression procedure.

Constrained nonlinear regression uses the algorithms proposed and implemented in NPSOL® by Gill, Murray, Saunders, and Wright to estimate the model parameters.

Example. Can population be predicted based on time? A scatterplot shows that there seems to be a strong relationship between population and time, but the relationship is nonlinear, so it requires the special estimation methods of the Nonlinear Regression procedure. By setting up an appropriate equation, such as a logistic population growth model, we can get a good estimate of the model, allowing us to make predictions about population for times that were not actually measured.

Statistics. For each iteration: parameter estimates and residual sum of squares. For each model: sum of squares for regression, residual, uncorrected total and corrected total, parameter estimates, asymptotic standard errors, and asymptotic correlation matrix of parameter estimates.

Data. The dependent and independent variables should be quantitative. Categorical variables such as religion, major, or region of residence need to be recoded to binary (dummy) variables or other types of contrast variables.

Assumptions. Results are valid only if you have specified a function that accurately describes the relationship between dependent and independent variables. Additionally, the choice of good starting values is very important. Even if you've specified the correct functional form of the model, if you use poor starting values, your model may fail to converge or you may get a locally optimal solution rather than one that is globally optimal.

Related procedures. Many models that appear nonlinear at first can be transformed to a linear model, which can be analyzed using the Linear Regression procedure. If you are uncertain what the proper model should be, the Curve Estimation procedure can help to identify useful functional relations in your data.

To Obtain a Nonlinear Regression Analysis

▶ From the menus choose:

Analyze
  Regression
    Nonlinear...

Figure 5.1   Nonlinear Regression dialog box

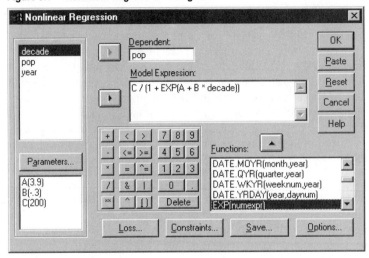

▶ Select one numeric dependent variable from the list of variables in your working data file.

▶ To build a model expression, enter the expression in the Model field or paste components (variables, parameters, functions) into the field.

▶ Identify parameters in your model by clicking *Parameters*.

A segmented model (one that takes different forms in different parts of its domain) must be specified by using *conditional logic* within the single model statement.

Conditional Logic (Nonlinear Regression)

You can specify a segmented model using conditional logic. To use conditional logic within a model expression or a loss function, you form the sum of a series of terms, one for each condition. Each term consists of a logical expression (in parentheses) multiplied by the expression that should result when that logical expression is true.

For example, consider a segmented model that equals 0 for $X <= 0$, X for $0 < X < 1$, and 1 for $X >= 1$. The expression for this is:

$(X <= 0)*0 + (X > 0 \ \& \ X < 1)*X + (X >= 1)*1.$

The logical expressions in parentheses all evaluate to 1 (true) or 0 (false). Therefore:

If $X <= 0$, the above reduces to $1*0 + 0*X + 0*1 = 0$.

If $0 < X < 1$, it reduces to $0*0 + 1*X + 0*1 = X$.

If $X >= 1$, it reduces to $0*0 + 0*X + 1*1 = 1$.

More complicated examples can be easily built by substituting different logical expressions and outcome expressions. Remember that double inequalities, such as $0 < X < 1$, must be written as compound expressions, such as $(X > 0 \ \& \ X < 1)$.

String variables can be used within logical expressions:

(city = 'New York')*costliv + (city = 'Des Moines')*0.59*costliv

This yields one expression (the value of the variable *costliv*) for New Yorkers and another (59% of that value) for Des Moines residents. String constants must be enclosed in quotation marks or apostrophes, as shown here.

Nonlinear Regression Parameters

Figure 5.2   Nonlinear Regression Parameters dialog box

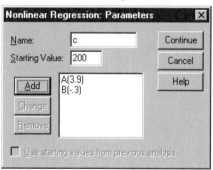

Parameters are the parts of your model that the Nonlinear Regression procedure estimates. Parameters can be additive constants, multiplicative coefficients, exponents, or values used in evaluating functions. All parameters that you have defined will appear (with their initial values) on the Parameters list in the main dialog box.

Name. You must specify a name for each parameter. This name must be a valid SPSS variable name and must be the name used in the model expression in the main dialog box.

Starting Value. Allows you to specify a starting value for the parameter, preferably as close as possible to the expected final solution. Poor starting values can result in failure to converge or in convergence on a solution that is local (rather than global) or is physically impossible.

Use starting values from previous analysis. If you have already run a nonlinear regression from this dialog box, you can select this option to obtain the initial values of parameters from their values in the previous run. This permits you to continue searching when the algorithm is converging slowly. (The initial starting values will still appear on the Parameters list in the main dialog box.) *Note:* This selection persists in this dialog box for the rest of your session. *If you change the model, be sure to deselect it.*

Nonlinear Regression Common Models

The table below provides example model syntax for many published nonlinear regression models. *A model selected at random is not likely to fit your data well.* Appropriate starting values for the parameters are necessary, and some models require constraints in order to converge.

Table 5.1   Example model syntax

Name	Model expression
Asymptotic Regression	b1 + b2 *exp(b3 * x)
Asymptotic Regression	b1 –(b2 *(b3 ** x))
Density	(b1 + b2 * x)**(–1/ b3)
Gauss	b1 *(1– b3 *exp(–b2 * x **2))
Gompertz	b1 *exp(–b2 * exp(–b3 * x))
Johnson-Schumacher	b1 *exp(–b2 / (x + b3))
Log-Modified	(b1 + b3 * x) ** b2
Log-Logistic	b1 –ln(1+ b2 *exp(–b3 * x))
Metcherlich Law of Diminishing Returns	b1 + b2 *exp(–b3 * x)
Michaelis Menten	b1* x /(x + b2)
Morgan-Mercer-Florin	(b1 * b2 + b3 * x ** b4)/(b2 + x ** b4)
Peal-Reed	b1 /(1+ b2 *exp(–(b3 * x + b4 * x **2+ b5 * x **3)))
Ratio of Cubics	(b1 + b2 * x + b3 * x **2+ b4 * x **3)/(b5 * x **3)
Ratio of Quadratics	(b1 + b2 * x + b3 * x **2)/(b4 * x **2)
Richards	b1 /((1+ b3 *exp(– b2 * x))**(1/ b4))
Verhulst	b1 /(1 + b3 * exp(– b2 * x))
Von Bertalanffy	(b1 ** (1 – b4) – b2 * exp(–b3 * x)) ** (1/(1 – b4))
Weibull	b1 – b2 *exp(– b3 * x ** b4)
Yield Density	(b1 + b2 * x + b3 * x **2)**(–1)

Nonlinear Regression Loss Function

Figure 5.3   Nonlinear Regression Loss Function dialog box

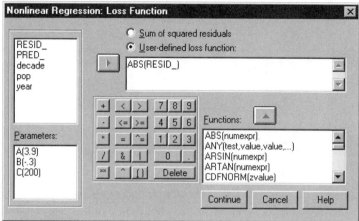

The **loss function** in nonlinear regression is the function that is minimized by the algorithm. Select either *Sum of squared residuals* to minimize the sum of the squared residuals or *User-defined loss function* to minimize a different function.

If you select *User-defined loss function*, you must define the loss function whose sum (across all cases) should be minimized by the choice of parameter values.

• Most loss functions involve the special variable *RESID_*, which represents the residual. (The default *Sum of squared residuals* loss function could be entered explicitly as RESID_**2.) If you need to use the predicted value in your loss function, it is equal to the dependent variable minus the residual.

• It is possible to specify a *conditional loss function* using conditional logic.

You can either type an expression in the User-defined loss function field or paste components of the expression into the field. String constants must be enclosed in quotation marks or apostrophes, and numeric constants must be typed in American format, with the dot as a decimal delimiter.

Nonlinear Regression Parameter Constraints

Figure 5.4   Nonlinear Regression Parameter Constraints dialog box

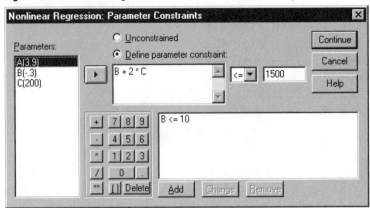

A **constraint** is a restriction on the allowable values for a parameter during the iterative search for a solution. Linear expressions are evaluated before a step is taken, so you can use linear constraints to prevent steps that might result in overflows. Nonlinear expressions are evaluated after a step is taken.

Each equation or inequality requires the following elements:

- An expression *involving at least one parameter* in the model. Type the expression or use the keypad, which allows you to paste numbers, operators, or parentheses into the expression. You can either type in the required parameter(s) along with the rest of the expression or paste from the Parameters list at the left. You cannot use ordinary variables in a constraint.

- One of the three logical operators <=, =, or >=.

- A numeric constant, to which the expression is compared using the logical operator. Type the constant. Numeric constants must be typed in American format, with the dot as a decimal delimiter.

Nonlinear Regression Save New Variables

Figure 5.5   Nonlinear Regression Save New Variables dialog box

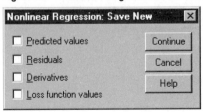

You can save a number of new variables to your active data file. Available options are Predicted values, Residuals, Derivatives, and Loss function values. These variables can be used in subsequent analyses to test the fit of the model or to identify problem cases.

Nonlinear Regression Options

Figure 5.6   Nonlinear Regression Options dialog box

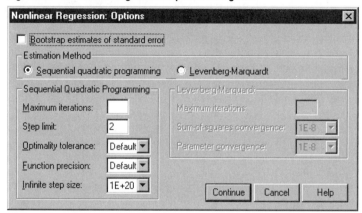

Options allow you to control various aspects of your nonlinear regression analysis:

Bootstrap estimates of standard error. Requests bootstrap estimates of the standard errors for parameters. This requires the sequential quadratic programming algorithm.

Estimation Method. Allows you to select an estimation method, if possible. (Certain choices in this or other dialog boxes require the sequential quadratic programming algorithm.) Available alternatives include Sequential quadratic programming and Levenberg-Marquardt.

Sequential Quadratic Programming. Allows you to specify options for this estimation method. You can enter new values for Maximum iterations and Step limit, and you can change the selection in the drop-down lists for Optimality tolerance, Function precision, and Infinite step size.

Levenberg-Marquardt. Allows you to specify options for this estimation process. You can enter new values for Maximum iterations, and you can change the selection in the drop-down lists for Sum-of-squares convergence and Parameter convergence.

Interpreting Nonlinear Regression Results

Nonlinear regression problems often present computational difficulties:

- The choice of initial values for the parameters influences convergence. Try to choose initial values that are reasonable and, if possible, close to the expected final solution.

- Sometimes one algorithm performs better than the other on a particular problem. In the Options dialog box, select the other algorithm if it is available. (If you specify a loss function or certain types of constraints, you cannot use the Levenberg-Marquardt algorithm.)

- When iteration stops only because the maximum number of iterations has occurred, the "final" model is probably not a good solution. Select *Use starting values from previous analysis* in the Parameters dialog box to continue the iteration or, better yet, choose different initial values.

- Models that require exponentiation of or by large data values can cause overflows or underflows (numbers too large or too small for the computer to represent). Sometimes you can avoid these by suitable choice of initial values or by imposing constraints on the parameters.

NLR Command Additional Features

The SPSS command language also allows you to:

- Name a file from which to read initial values for parameter estimates.

- Specify more than one model statement and loss function. This makes it easier to specify a segmented model.

- Supply your own derivatives rather than use those calculated by the program.

- Specify the number of bootstrap samples to generate.

- Specify additional iteration criteria, including setting a critical value for derivative checking and defining a convergence criterion for the correlation between the residuals and the derivatives.

Additional criteria for the CNLR (constrained nonlinear regression) command allow you to:

- Specify the maximum number of minor iterations allowed within each major iteration.

- Set a critical value for derivative checking.

- Set a step limit.

- Specify a crash tolerance to determine if initial values are within their specified bounds.

6 Weight Estimation

Standard linear regression models assume that variance is constant within the population under study. When this is not the case—for example, when cases that are high on some attribute show more variability than cases that are low on that attribute—linear regression using ordinary least squares (OLS) no longer provides optimal model estimates. If the differences in variability can be predicted from another variable, the Weight Estimation procedure can compute the coefficients of a linear regression model using weighted least squares (WLS), such that the more precise observations (that is, those with less variability) are given greater weight in determining the regression coefficients. The Weight Estimation procedure tests a range of weight transformations and indicates which will give the best fit to the data.

Example. What are the effects of inflation and unemployment on changes in stock prices? Because stocks with higher share values often show more variability than those with low share values, ordinary least squares will not produce optimal estimates. Weight estimation allows you to account for the effect of share price on the variability of price changes in calculating the linear model.

Statistics. Log-likelihood values for each power of the weight source variable tested, multiple R, R-squared, adjusted R-squared, ANOVA table for WLS model, unstandardized and standardized parameter estimates, and log-likelihood for the WLS model.

Data. The dependent and independent variables should be quantitative. Categorical variables such as religion, major, or region of residence need to be recoded to binary (dummy) variables or other types of contrast variables. The weight variable should be quantitative and should be related to the variability in the dependent variable.

Assumptions. For each value of the independent variable, the distribution of the dependent variable must be normal. The relationship between the dependent variable and each independent variable should be linear, and all observations should be independent. The variance of the dependent variable can vary across levels of the independent variable(s), but the differences must be predictable based on the weight variable.

Related procedures. The Explore procedure can be used to screen your data. Explore provides tests for normality and homogeneity of variance, as well as graphical displays. If your dependent variable seems to have equal variance across levels of independent variables, you can use the Linear Regression procedure. If your data appear to violate an assumption (such as normality), try transforming them. If your data are not related linearly and a transformation does not help, use an alternate model in the Curve Estimation procedure. If your dependent variable is dichotomous—for example, whether a particular sale is completed or whether an item is defective—use the Logistic Regression procedure. If your dependent variable is censored—for example, survival time after surgery—use Life Tables, Kaplan-Meier, or Cox Regression, available in the SPSS Advanced Models option. If your data are not independent—for example, if you observe the same person under several conditions—use the Repeated Measures procedure, available in the SPSS Advanced Models option.

To Obtain a Weight Estimation Analysis

▶ From the menus choose:

Analyze
  Regression
    Weight Estimation...

Figure 6.1   Weight Estimation dialog box

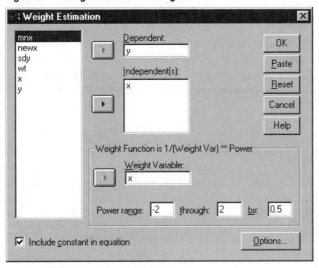

▶ Select one dependent variable.

▶ Select one or more independent variables.

▶ Select the variable that is the source of heteroscedasticity as the weight variable.

Weight Estimation Options

Figure 6.2   Weight Estimation Options dialog box

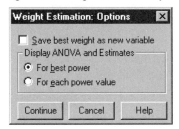

You can specify options for your weight estimation analysis:

Save best weight as new variable. Adds the weight variable to the active file. This variable is called *WGT_n*, where *n* is a number chosen to give the variable a unique name.

Display ANOVA and Estimates. Allows you to control how statistics are displayed in the output. Available alternatives are For best power and For each power value.

WLS Command Additional Features

The SPSS command language also allows you to:

• Provide a single value for the power.

• Specify a list of power values, or mix a range of values with a list of values for the power.

7 Two-Stage Least-Squares Regression

Standard linear regression models assume that errors in the dependent variable are uncorrelated with the independent variable(s). When this is not the case (for example, when relationships between variables are bidirectional), linear regression using ordinary least squares (OLS) no longer provides optimal model estimates. Two-stage least-squares regression uses instrumental variables that are uncorrelated with the error terms to compute estimated values of the problematic predictor(s) (the first stage), and then uses those computed values to estimate a linear regression model of the dependent variable (the second stage). Since the computed values are based on variables that are uncorrelated with the errors, the results of the two-stage model are optimal.

Example. Is the demand for a commodity related to its price and consumers' incomes? The difficulty in this model is that price and demand have a reciprocal effect on each other. That is, price can influence demand and demand can also influence price. A two-stage least-squares regression model might use consumers' incomes and lagged price to calculate a proxy for price that is uncorrelated with the measurement errors in demand. This proxy is substituted for price itself in the originally specified model, which is then estimated.

Statistics. For each model: standardized and unstandardized regression coefficients, multiple R, R-squared, adjusted R-squared, standard error of the estimate, analysis-of-variance table, predicted values, and residuals. Also, 95% confidence intervals for each regression coefficient, and correlation and covariance matrices of parameter estimates.

Data. The dependent and independent variables should be quantitative. Categorical variables, such as religion, major, or region of residence, need to be recoded to binary (dummy) variables or other types of contrast variables. Endogenous explanatory variables should be quantitative (not categorical).

Assumptions. For each value of the independent variable, the distribution of the dependent variable must be normal. The variance of the distribution of the dependent variable should be constant for all values of the independent variable. The relationship between the dependent variable and each independent variable should be linear.

Related procedures. If you believe that none of your predictor variables is correlated with the errors in your dependent variable, you can use the Linear Regression procedure. If your data appear to violate one of the assumptions (such as normality or constant variance), try transforming them. If your data are not related linearly and a transformation

31

does not help, use an alternate model in the Curve Estimation procedure. If your dependent variable is dichotomous, such as whether a particular sale is completed or not, use the Logistic Regression procedure. If your data are not independent—for example, if you observe the same person under several conditions—use the Repeated Measures procedure, available in the SPSS Advanced Models option.

To Obtain a Two-Stage Least-Squares Regression Analysis

▶ From the menus choose:

Analyze
  Regression
    2-Stage Least Squares...

Figure 7.1   2-Stage Least Squares dialog box

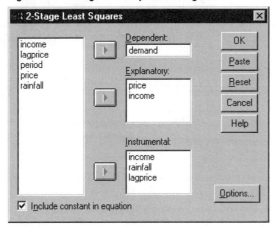

▶ Select one dependent variable.

▶ Select one or more explanatory (predictor) variables.

▶ Select one or more instrumental variables.

Explanatory variables not specified as instrumental are considered endogenous. Normally, all of the exogenous variables in the Explanatory list are also specified as instrumental variables.

Two-Stage Least-Squares Regression Options

Figure 7.2   2-Stage Least Squares Options dialog box

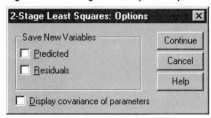

You can select the following options for your analysis:

Save New Variables. Allows you to add new variables to your active file. Available options are Predicted and Residuals.

Display covariance of parameters. Allows you to print the covariance matrix of the parameter estimates.

2SLS Command Additional Features

The SPSS command language also allows you to estimate multiple equations simultaneously.

8 Logistic Regression Analysis Examples

Predicting whether an event will or will not occur, as well as identifying the variables useful in making the prediction, is important in most academic disciplines and in the "real" world. Why do some citizens vote and others do not? Why do some people develop coronary heart disease and others do not? Why do some businesses succeed and others fail?

A variety of multivariate statistical techniques can be used to predict a binary dependent variable from a set of independent variables. Multiple regression analysis and discriminant analysis are two related techniques that quickly come to mind. However, these techniques pose difficulties when the dependent variable can have only two values—an event occurring or not occurring.

When the dependent variable can have only two values, the assumptions necessary for hypothesis testing in regression analysis are necessarily violated. For example, it is unreasonable to assume that the distribution of errors is normal. Another difficulty with multiple regression analysis is that predicted values cannot be interpreted as probabilities. They are not constrained to fall in the interval between 0 and 1.

Linear discriminant analysis does allow direct prediction of group membership, but the assumption of multivariate normality of the independent variables, as well as equal variance-covariance matrices in the two groups, is required for the prediction rule to be optimal.

In this chapter, we will consider another multivariate technique for estimating the probability that an event occurs—the **binary logistic regression model**. This model requires far fewer assumptions than discriminant analysis; and even when the assumptions required for discriminant analysis are satisfied, logistic regression still performs well. (See Hosmer and Lemeshow, 1989, or Kleinbaum, 1994, for an introduction to logistic regression.)

Extension of the binary logistic regression model to response variables with more than two categories, multinomial logistic regression, is discussed in Chapter 9. The multinomial logistic regression procedure can also be used to fit a conditional logistic regression model for matched case control pairs, as well as binary logistic regression models. See Chapter 1 for a comparison of the features available in the two logistic regression procedures.

The Logistic Regression Model

In logistic regression, you directly estimate the probability of an event occurring. For the case of a single independent variable, the logistic regression model can be written as

$$\text{Prob (event)} = \frac{e^{B_0 + B_1 X}}{1 + e^{B_0 + B_1 X}} \qquad \qquad \textbf{Equation 8.1}$$

or equivalently

$$\text{Prob (event)} = \frac{1}{1 + e^{-(B_0 + B_1 X)}} \qquad \qquad \textbf{Equation 8.2}$$

where B_0 and B_1 are coefficients estimated from the data, X is the independent variable, and e is the base of the natural logarithms, approximately 2.718.

For more than one independent variable, the model can be written as

$$\text{Prob (event)} = \frac{e^Z}{1 + e^Z} \qquad \qquad \textbf{Equation 8.3}$$

or equivalently

$$\text{Prob (event)} = \frac{1}{1 + e^{-Z}} \qquad \qquad \textbf{Equation 8.4}$$

where Z is the linear combination

$$Z = B_0 + B_1 X_1 + B_2 X_2 + ... + B_p X_p \qquad \qquad \textbf{Equation 8.5}$$

and p is the number of independent variables.

The probability of the event not occurring is estimated as

$$\text{Prob(no event)} = 1 - \text{Prob(event)} \qquad \qquad \textbf{Equation 8.6}$$

Figure 8.1 is a plot of a logistic regression curve when the values of Z are between −5 and +5. As you can see, the curve is S-shaped. It closely resembles the curve obtained when the cumulative probability of the normal distribution is plotted. The relationship between the independent variable and the probability is nonlinear. The probability estimates will always be between 0 and 1, regardless of the value of Z.

Figure 8.1   Plot of logistic regression curve

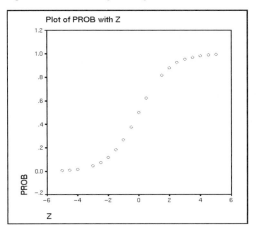

In linear regression, we estimate the parameters of the model using the **least-squares method**. That is, we select regression coefficients that result in the smallest sums of squared distances between the observed and the predicted values of the dependent variable.

In logistic regression, the parameters of the model are estimated using the **maximum-likelihood method**. That is, the coefficients that make our observed results most likely are selected. Since the logistic regression model is nonlinear, an iterative algorithm is necessary for parameter estimation.

An Example

The treatment and prognosis of cancer depends on how much the disease has spread. One of the regions to which a cancer may spread is the lymph nodes. If the lymph nodes are involved, the prognosis is generally poorer than if they are not. That's why it's desirable to establish as early as possible whether the lymph nodes are cancerous. For certain cancers, exploratory surgery is done just to determine whether the nodes are cancerous, since this will determine what treatment is needed. If we could predict whether the nodes are affected or not on the basis of data that can be obtained without performing surgery, considerable discomfort and expense could be avoided.

For this chapter, we will use data presented by Brown (1980) for 53 men with prostate cancer. For each patient, he reports the age, serum acid phosphatase (a laboratory value that is elevated if the tumor has spread to certain areas), the stage of the disease (an indication of how advanced the disease is), the grade of the tumor (an indication of aggressiveness), and X-ray results, as well as whether the cancer had spread to the regional lymph nodes at the time of surgery. The problem is to predict whether the nodes are positive for cancer based on the values of the variables that can be measured without surgery.

Coefficients for the Logistic Model

Figure 8.2 contains the estimated coefficients (under column heading *B*) and related statistics from the logistic regression model that predicts nodal involvement from a constant and the variables *age*, *acid*, *xray*, *stage*, and *grade*. The last three of these variables (*xray*, *stage*, and *grade*) are **indicator variables**, coded 0 or 1. The value of 1 for *xray* indicates positive X-ray findings, the value of 1 for *stage* indicates advanced stage, and the value of 1 for *grade* indicates a more aggressively spreading malignant tumor.

Figure 8.2   Parameter estimates for the logistic regression model

Variables in the Equation

	B	S.E.	Wald	df	Sig.	Exp(B)	95.0% C.I.for EXP(B) Lower	Upper
ACID	.024	.013	3.423	1	.064	1.025	.999	1.051
AGE	-.069	.058	1.432	1	.231	.933	.833	1.045
XRAY	2.045	.807	6.421	1	.011	7.732	1.589	37.614
STAGE	1.564	.774	4.083	1	.043	4.778	1.048	21.783
GRADE	.761	.771	.976	1	.323	2.141	.473	9.700
Constant	.062	3.460	.000	1	.986	1.064		

Given these coefficients, the logistic regression equation for the probability of nodal involvement can be written as

$$\text{Prob (nodal involvement)} = \frac{1}{1 + e^{-Z}}$$

Equation 8.7

where

$$Z = 0.0618 - 0.0693(\text{age}) + 0.0243(\text{acid}) + 2.0453(\text{xray})$$
$$+ 0.7614(\text{grade}) + 1.5641(\text{stage})$$

Equation 8.8

Applying this to a man who is 66 years old, with a serum acid phosphatase level of 48 and values of 0 for the remaining independent variables, we find

$$Z = 0.0618 - 0.0693(66) + 0.0243(48) = -3.346$$

Equation 8.9

The probability of nodal involvement is then estimated to be

$$\text{Prob (nodal involvement)} = \frac{1}{1 + e^{-(-3.346)}} = 0.0340 \qquad \textbf{Equation 8.10}$$

Based on this estimate, we would predict that the nodes are unlikely to be malignant. In general, if the estimated probability of the event is less than 0.5, we predict that the event will not occur. If the probability is greater than 0.5, we predict that the event will occur. (In the unlikely event that the probability is exactly 0.5, we can flip a coin for our prediction.)

However, the decision as to what probability cutoff to actually use for predicting that nodes are positive depends on the consequences of failing to correctly identify patients with positive nodes as compared to the consequences of falsely identifying patients as having positive nodes.

Testing Hypotheses about the Coefficients

For large sample sizes, the test that a coefficient is 0 can be based on the **Wald statistic**, which has a chi-square distribution. When a variable has a single degree of freedom, the Wald statistic is just the square of the ratio of the coefficient to its standard error.

For categorical variables with more than one degree of freedom, an overall Wald statistic with degrees of freedom equal to one less than the number of categories is also calculated. The overall Wald statistic is

$$W = B'V^{-1}B$$

where B is the vector of maximum likelihood estimates for the coefficients of the categorical variable and V^{-1} is the inverse of the asymptotic variance covariance matrix of the coefficients.

For example, the coefficient for age is -0.0693, and its standard error is 0.0579. (The standard errors for the logistic regression coefficients are shown in the column labeled *S.E.* in Figure 8.2.) The Wald statistic is $(-0.0693/0.0579)^2$, or about 1.432. The significance level for the Wald statistic is shown in the column labeled *Sig*. In this example, only the coefficients for *xray* and *stage* appear to be significantly different from 0, using a significance level of 0.05.

Unfortunately, the Wald statistic has a very undesirable property. When the absolute value of the regression coefficient becomes large, the estimated standard error is too large. This produces a Wald statistic that is too small, leading you to fail to reject the null hypothesis that the coefficient is 0, when in fact you should. Therefore, whenever you have a large coefficient, you should not rely on the Wald statistic for hypothesis testing. Instead, you should build a model with and without that variable and base your hypothesis test on the change in the log-likelihood (Hauck and Donner, 1977). It is a good idea to examine the change in the log-likelihood when each of the variables is entered into an equation containing the other variables. You can do this by selecting Backward LR as the method for variable selection and specifying the probability level for removal as 1.

Interpreting the Regression Coefficients

In multiple linear regression, the interpretation of the regression coefficient is straight-forward. It tells you the amount of change in the dependent variable for a one-unit change in the independent variable.

To understand the interpretation of the logistic coefficients, consider a rearrangement of the equation for the logistic model. The logistic model can be rewritten in terms of the odds of an event occurring. (The **odds** of an event occurring are defined as the ratio of the probability that it will occur to the probability that it will not. For example, the odds of getting a head on a single flip of a coin are $0.5/0.5 = 1$. Similarly, the odds of getting a diamond on a single draw from a card deck are $0.25/0.75 = 1/3$. Don't confuse this technical meaning of odds with its informal usage to mean simply the probability.)

First let's write the logistic model in terms of the log of the odds, which is called a **logit**:

$$\log\left(\frac{\text{Prob(event)}}{\text{Prob(no event)}}\right) = B_0 + B_1 X_1 + \ldots + B_p X_p \qquad \textbf{Equation 8.11}$$

From Equation 8.11, you see that the logistic coefficient can be interpreted as the change in the log odds associated with a one-unit change in the independent variable. For exam-ple, from Figure 8.2, you see that the coefficient for *grade* is 0.76. This tells you that when the grade changes from 0 to 1 and the values of the other independent variables remain the same, the log odds of the nodes being malignant increase by 0.76.

Since it's easier to think of odds rather than log odds, the logistic equation can be written in terms of odds as

$$\frac{\text{Prob (event)}}{\text{Prob (no event)}} = e^{B_0 + B_1 X_1 + \ldots + B_p X_p} = e^{B_0} e^{B_1 X_1} \ldots e^{B_p X_p} \qquad \textbf{Equation 8.12}$$

Then e raised to the power B_i is the factor by which the odds change when the ith inde-pendent variable increases by one unit. (This is true only if the ith variable is not included in any other variables such as interactions.) If B_i is positive, this factor will be greater than 1, which means that the odds are increased; if B_i is negative, the factor will be less than 1, which means that the odds are decreased. When B_i is 0, the factor equals 1, which leaves the odds unchanged. For example, when *grade* changes from 0 to 1, the odds are increased by a factor of 2.14, as is shown in the *Exp(B)* column in Figure 8.2.

As a further example, let's calculate the odds of having malignant nodes for a 60-year-old man with a serum acid phosphatase level of 62, a value of 1 for X-ray results, and values of 0 for stage and grade of tumor. First, calculate the probability that the nodes are malignant:

$$\text{Estimated prob (malignant nodes)} = \frac{1}{1 + e^{-Z}} \qquad \textbf{Equation 8.13}$$

where

$$Z = 0.0618 - 0.0693(60) + 0.0243(62) + 2.0453(1)$$
$$+ 0.7614(0) + (1.5641)(0) = -0.54 \qquad \textbf{Equation 8.14}$$

The estimated probability of malignant nodes is therefore 0.37. The probability of not having malignant nodes is 0.63 (that is, $1 - 0.37$). The *odds* of having a malignant node are then estimated as

$$\text{Odds} = \frac{\text{Prob (event)}}{\text{Prob (no event)}} = \frac{0.37}{1 - 0.37} = 0.59 \qquad \textbf{Equation 8.15}$$

and the log odds are –0.53.

What would be the probability of malignant nodes if, instead of 0, the case had a value of 1 for *grade*? Following the same procedure as before, but using a value of 1 for *grade*, the estimated probability of malignant nodes is 0.554. Similarly, the estimated odds are 1.24, and the log odds are 0.22.

By increasing the value of *grade* by one unit, we have increased the log odds by about 0.75, the value of the coefficient for *grade*. (Since we didn't use many digits in our hand calculations, our value of 0.75 isn't exactly equal to the 0.76 value for *grade* shown in Figure 8.2. If we carried the computations out with enough precision, we would arrive at exactly the value of the coefficient.)

By increasing the value of *grade* from 0 to 1, the odds changed from 0.59 to 1.24. The ratio of the odds of positive nodes when *grade* is 1 to the same odds when *grade* is 0 is about 2.1. This ratio is called the **odds ratio**. The odds ratio for a variable tells you change in odds for a case when the value of that variable increases by 1. The odds ratio for *grade* is in the column labeled *Exp(B)* in Figure 8.2. Its 95% confidence interval is in the last two columns of Figure 8.2. From the 95% confidence interval, you can see that values anywhere from 0.47 to 9.7 are plausible for the population value of the odds ratio for *grade*. Since this interval includes the value 1—no change in odds—you can't conclude based on this sample of data that a unit change in *grade* in the population is associated with a change in the odds of positive nodes. (Since the confidence interval for the odds ratio is based on the confidence interval for the corresponding logistic regression coefficient, the confidence interval for the odds ratio will include 1 whenever the confidence interval for the regression coefficient contains 0.)

When an independent variable is continuous, such as age, blood pressure, or years of education, the odds ratio for a unit change in the value of the independent variable may be less informative than the odds ratio associated with a decade change in age, or a 5 mm change in blood pressure. The odds ratio for a change of C units is e^{CB}, where B is the coefficient for a change of one unit.

Assessing the Goodness of Fit of the Model

Whenever you fit a model to data, you want to know how well the model fits not only the sample of data from which it is derived, but also the population from which the sample data were selected. A model almost always fits the sample you used to estimate it better than it will fit the population. For large data sets, it may be feasible to split the data into two parts. You can estimate a model on one part and then apply the model to the other to see how well it fits. There are also other statistical techniques with picturesque names such as "jackknifing" and "bootstrapping" that are useful for assessing how well the model would fit another set of data.

Two additional criteria for evaluating model performance in logistic regression are called model discrimination and model calibration. **Model discrimination** evaluates the ability of the model to distinguish between the two groups of cases, based on the estimated probability of the event occurring. That is, you want to know how well the predicted probabilities of the event occurring separate the cases for whom the outcome actually occurs and those for whom it does not. **Model calibration** evaluates how well the observed and predicted probabilities agree over the entire range of probability values. Let's first consider some simple ways to examine model discrimination. "Another Look at Model Fit" on p. 61 continues this topic by presenting summary measures of model discrimination and calibration.

The Classification Table

One way to assess how well our model fits is to compare our predictions to the observed outcomes. Figure 8.3 compares the observed and predicted group memberships when cases with a predicted probability of 0.5 or greater are classified as having positive nodes.

Figure 8.3   Classification table

Classification Table [1]

Observed		Predicted		
		NODES		Percentage Correct
		Neg	Pos	
NODES	Neg	28	5	84.8
	Pos	7	13	65.0
Overall Percentage				77.4

[1]. The cut value is .500

From the table, you see that 28 patients without malignant nodes were correctly predicted by the model not to have malignant nodes. Similarly, 13 men with positive nodes were correctly predicted to have positive nodes. The off-diagonal entries of the table tell you how many men were incorrectly classified. A total of 12 men were misclassified in this example—5 men with negative nodes and 7 men with positive nodes. Of the men without diseased nodes, 84.8% were correctly classified. Of the men with diseased nodes, 65% were correctly classified. Overall, 77.4% of the 53 men were correctly classified.

The classification table doesn't reveal the distribution of estimated probabilities for men in the two groups. For each predicted group, the table shows only whether the estimated probability is greater or less than one-half. For example, you cannot tell from the table whether the seven patients who had false negative results had predicted probabilities near 50%, or low predicted probabilities. Ideally, you would like the two groups to have very different estimated probabilities. That is, you would like to see small estimated probabilities of positive nodes for all men without malignant nodes and large estimated probabilities for all men with malignant nodes.

Histogram of Estimated Probabilities

Figure 8.4 is a histogram of the estimated probabilities of cancerous nodes. The symbol used for each case designates the group to which the case actually belongs. If you have a model that successfully distinguishes the two groups, the cases for which the event has occurred should be to the right of 0.5, while the cases for which the event has not occurred should be to the left of 0.5. The more the two groups cluster at their respective ends of the plot, the better.

Figure 8.4   Histogram of estimated probabilities

```
                    Observed Groups and Predicted Probabilities

            4 +  NN                                                        +
            I    NN                                                        I
            I    NN                                                        I
F           I    NN                                                        I
R           3 +  NN    P            P                             P        +
E           I    NN    P            P                             P        I
Q           I    NN    P            P                             P        I
U           I    NN    P            P                             P        I
E           2 +  NNNN  N   PP       N        P    PP              P    P   +
N           I    NNNN  N   PP       N        P    PP              P    P   I
C           I    NNNN  N   PP       N        P    PP              P    P   I
Y           I    NNNN  N   PP       N        P    PP              P    P   I
            1 +  NNNNNNNPNNNN NNPNN    N    NN NNN N      P P   P P P NP PP +
            I    NNNNNNNPNNNN NNPNN    N    NN NNN N      P P   P P P NP PP I
            I    NNNNNNNPNNNN NNPNN    N    NN NNN N      P P   P P P NP PP I
            I    NNNNNNNPNNNN NNPNN    N    NN NNN N      P P   P P P NP PP I
Predicted  --------------+--------------+--------------+--------------
  Prob:    0            .25            .5            .75            1
  Group:   NNNNNNNNNNNNNNNNNNNNNNNNNNNNNNNNNNNNPPPPPPPPPPPPPPPPPPPPPPPPPPPPPPPPPPPP

            Predicted Probability is of Membership for Pos
            The Cut Value is .50
            Symbols: N - Neg
                     P - Pos
            Each Symbol Represents .25 Cases.
```

From Figure 8.4, you see that there is only one noncancerous case with a high estimated probability of having positive nodes (the case identified with the letter *N* at a probability value of about 0.88). However, there are four diseased cases with estimated probabilities less than 0.25.

By looking at this histogram of predicted probabilities, you can see whether a different rule for assigning cases to groups might be useful. For example, if most of the misclassifications occur in the region around 0.5, you might decide to withhold judgment for cases with values in this region. In this example, this means that you would predict nodal involvement only for cases where you were reasonably sure that the logistic prediction would be correct. You might decide to operate on all questionable cases.

If the consequences of misclassification are not the same in both directions (for example, calling nodes negative when they are really positive is worse than calling nodes positive when they are really negative), the classification rule can be altered to decrease the possibility of making the more severe error. For example, you might decide to call cases "negative" only if their estimated probability is less than 0.3. By looking at the histogram of the estimated probabilities, you can get some idea of how different classification rules might perform. (Of course, when you apply the model to new cases, you can't expect the classification rule to behave exactly the same.)

Goodness of Fit of the Model

Seeing how well the model classifies the observed data is one way of determining how well the logistic model performs. Another way of assessing the goodness of fit of the model is to examine how "likely" the sample results actually are, given the parameter estimates. (Recall that we chose parameter estimates that would make our observed results as likely as possible.)

The probability of the observed results, given the parameter estimates, is known as the **likelihood**. Since the likelihood is a small number less than 1, it is customary to use -2 times the log of the likelihood ($-2LL$) as a measure of how well the estimated model fits the data. A good model is one that results in a high likelihood of the observed results. This translates to a small value for $-2LL$. (If a model fits perfectly, the likelihood is 1, and -2 times the log-likelihood is 0.) The change in the likelihood value is used to determine how the fit of a model changes as variables are added or deleted from a model.

For the logistic regression model that contains only the constant, $-2LL$ is 70.25, as shown in Figure 8.5, the iteration history. From this table, you can see how the estimates of the coefficients change at each iteration. (The $-2LL$ values calculated by the

Figure 8.5 $-2LL$ for model containing only the constant

Iteration History [1,2,3]

Iteration		-2 Log likelihood	Coefficients Constant
Step 0	1	70.253	-.491
	2	70.252	-.501

[1.] Constant is included in the model.

[2.] Initial -2 Log Likelihood: 70.252

[3.] Estimation terminated at iteration number 2 because Log-Likelihood decreased by less than .010 percent.

binary logistic regression procedure do not include the multinomial constant. They are kernel values.)

Goodness of Fit with All Variables

Figure 8.6 shows model summary statistics for the model with all of the independent variables. For the current model, the value of $-2LL$ is 48.126, which is smaller than the $-2LL$ for the model containing only a constant. The next two entries, the *Cox & Snell R^2* and the *Nagelkerke R^2*, are statistics that attempt to quantify the proportion of explained "variation" in the logistic regression model. They are similar in intent to the R^2 in a linear regression model, although the variation in a logistic regression model must be defined differently.

Figure 8.6   Model summary statistics

Model Summary

Step	-2 Log likelihood	Cox & Snell R Square	Nagelkerke R Square
1	48.126	.341	.465

The Cox and Snell R^2 is

$$R^2 = 1 - \left[\frac{L(0)}{L(B)}\right]^{2/N}$$

Equation 8.16

where $L(0)$ is the likelihood for the model with only a constant, $L(B)$ is the likelihood for the model under consideration, and N is the sample size. The problem with this measure for logistic regression is that it cannot achieve a maximum value of 1. Nagelkerke (1991) proposed a modification of the Cox and Snell R^2 so that the value of 1 could be achieved. The Nagelkerke $\tilde{R}^2$ is

$$\tilde{R}^2 = \frac{R^2}{R^2{}_{MAX}}$$

Equation 8.17

where $R^2{}_{MAX} = 1 - [L(0)]^{2/N}$

From the Nagelkerke $\tilde{R}^2$, you can see that about 47% of the "variation" in the outcome variable is explained by the logistic regression model.

Figure 8.7   Changes in –2LL

Improvement of Goodness-of-Fit

		Chi-square	df	Sig.
Step 1	Model	22.126	5	.000
	Block	22.126	5	.000
	Step	22.126	5	.000

There are three chi-square entries in Figure 8.7. They are labeled *Model, Block,* and *Step*. The model chi-square is the difference between $-2LL$ for the model with only a constant and $-2LL$ for the current model. (If a constant is not included in the model, the likelihood for the model without any variables is used for comparison.) Thus, the model chi-square tests the null hypothesis that the coefficients for all of the terms in the current model, except the constant, are 0. This is comparable to the overall F test for regression.

In this example, $-2LL$ for the model containing only the constant is 70.252 (from Figure 8.5), while for the complete model, it is 48.126. The model chi-square, 22.126, is the difference between these two values. The degrees of freedom for the model chi-square is the difference between the number of parameters in the two models.

The entry labeled *Block* is the change in $-2LL$ between successive entry blocks during model building (see "To Obtain a Logistic Regression Analysis" on p. 4 for information on entering variables in blocks). In this example, we entered our variables in a single block, so the block chi-square is the same as the model chi-square. If you enter variables in more than one block, the block chi-square provides a test of the null hypothesis that the coefficients for variables entered in the last block are zero.

The entry labeled *Step* is the change in $-2LL$ between successive steps of building a model. It tests the null hypothesis that the coefficients for the variables added at the last step are 0. In this example, we considered only two models: the constant-only model and the model with a constant and five independent variables. Thus, the model chi-square, the block chi-square, and the step chi-square values are all the same. If you sequentially consider more than just these two models, using either forward or backward variable selection, the block chi-square and step chi-square will differ. The step chi-square test is comparable to the F-change test in stepwise multiple regression.

Categorical Variables

In logistic regression, just as in linear regression, the codes for the independent variables must be meaningful. You cannot take a nominal variable, such as religion, assign arbitrary codes from 1 to 35, and then use the resulting variable in the model. In this situation, you must recode the values of the independent variable by creating a new set of variables that correspond in some way to the original categories.

If you have a two-category variable, such as sex, you can code each case as 0 or 1 to indicate either female or not female. Or, you could code it as being male or not male. This is called **dummy-variable** or **indicator-variable coding**. *Grade*, *stage*, and *xray* are all examples of two-category variables that have been coded as 0 and 1. The code of 1 indicates that the poorer outcome is present. The interpretation of the resulting coefficients for *grade*, *stage*, and *xray* is straightforward. It tells you the difference between the log odds when a case is a member of the "poor" category and when it is not.

When you have a variable with more than two categories, you must create new variables to represent the categories. The number of new variables required to represent a categorical variable is one less than the number of categories. For example, if instead of the actual values for serum acid phosphatase, you had values of 1, 2, or 3, depending on whether the value was low, medium, or high, you would have to create two new variables to represent the serum phosphatase effect. Two alternative coding schemes are described in "Indicator-Variable Coding Scheme" on p. 48 and "Another Coding Scheme" on p. 49.

Indicator-Variable Coding Scheme

One of the ways you can create two new variables for serum acid phosphatase is to use indicator variables to represent the categories. With this method, one variable would represent the low value, coded 1 if the value is low and 0 otherwise. The second variable would represent the medium value, coded 1 if the value is average and 0 otherwise. The value "high" would be represented by codes of 0 for both of these variables. The choice of the category to be coded as 0 for both variables is arbitrary.

With categorical variables, the only statement you can make about the effect of a particular category is in comparison to some other category. For example, if you have a variable that represents type of cancer, you can only make statements such as "lung cancer compared to bladder cancer decreases your chance of survival." Or you might say that "lung cancer compared to all the cancer types in the study decreases your chance of survival." You can't make a statement about lung cancer without relating it to the other types of cancer.

If you use indicator variables for coding, the coefficients for the new variables represent the effect of each category compared to a reference category. The coefficient for the reference category is 0. As an example, consider Figure 8.8. The variable *catacid1* is the indicator variable for low serum acid phosphatase, coded 1 for low levels and 0 otherwise. Similarly, the variable *catacid2* is the indicator variable for medium serum acid phosphatase. The reference category is high levels.

Figure 8.8   Indicator variables

Variables in the Equation

	B	S.E.	Wald	df	Sig.	Exp(B)
AGE	-.052	.063	.686	1	.407	.949
CATACID1	-2.008	1.052	3.643	1	.056	.134
CATACID2	-1.092	.926	1.390	1	.238	.335
XRAY	2.035	.837	5.903	1	.015	7.650
GRADE	.808	.823	.962	1	.327	2.243
STAGE	1.457	.768	3.597	1	.058	4.293
Constant	1.770	3.809	.216	1	.642	5.870

The coefficient for *catacid1* is the change in log odds when you have a low value compared to a high value. Similarly, *catacid2* is the change in log odds when you have a medium value compared to a high value. The coefficient for the high value is necessarily 0, since it does not differ from itself. In Figure 8.8, you see that the coefficients for both of the indicator variables are negative. This means that compared to high values for serum acid phosphatase, low and medium values are associated with decreased log odds of malignant nodes. The low category decreases the log odds more than the medium category.

The SPSS Logistic Regression procedure will automatically create new variables for variables declared as categorical (see "Logistic Regression Define Categorical Variables" on p. 5 in Chapter 2). You can choose the coding scheme you want to use for the new variables.

Figure 8.9 shows the table that is displayed for each categorical variable. The rows of the table correspond to the categories of the variable. The actual value is given in the column labeled *Value*. The number of cases with each value is displayed in the column labeled *Freq*. Subsequent columns correspond to new variables created by the program. The number in parentheses indicates the suffix used to identify the variable in the output. The codes that represent each original category using the new variables are listed under the corresponding new-variable column.

Figure 8.9   Indicator-variable coding scheme

Categorical Variable Encoding

Varvalue		Frequency	Parameter coding (1)	Parameter coding (2)
CATACID	1.00	15	1	0
	2.00	20	0	1
	3.00	18	0	0

From Figure 8.9, you see that there are 20 cases with a value of 2 for *catacid*. Each of these cases will be assigned a code of 0 for the new variable *catacid(1)* and a code of 1 for the new variable *catacid(2)*. Similarly, cases with a value of 3 for *catacid* will be given the code of 0 for both *catacid(1)* and *catacid(2)*.

Another Coding Scheme

The statement you can make based on the logistic regression coefficients depends on how you have created the new variables used to represent the categorical variable. As shown in the previous section, when you use indicator variables for coding, the coefficients for the new variables represent the effect of each category compared to a reference category. If, on the other hand, you wanted to compare the effect of each category to the average effect of all of the categories, you could have selected the deviation coding scheme shown in Figure 8.10. This differs from indicator-variable coding only in that the last category is coded as −1 for each of the new variables.

With this coding scheme, the logistic regression coefficients tell you how much better or worse each category is compared to the average effect of all categories, as shown in Figure 8.11. For each new variable, the coefficients now represent the difference from the average effect over all categories. The value of the coefficient for the last category is not displayed, but it is no longer 0. Instead, it is the negative of the sum of the displayed coefficients. From Figure 8.11, the coefficient for "high" level is calculated as $-(-0.9745 - 0.0589) = 1.0334$.

Figure 8.10   Deviation coding scheme

Categorical Variable Encoding

Varvalue		Frequency	Parameter coding	
			(1)	(2)
CATACID	1.00	15	1	0
	2.00	20	0	1
	3.00	18	-1	-1

Note that the parameter coding shown in Figure 8.10 tells you how the data values are transformed to obtain the specified type of parameter estimates. The parameter coding table shows you the linear combination of categories corresponding to each parameter estimate only if the contrasts that you specify are orthogonal. Since deviation contrasts are not orthogonal, the parameter coding shown in Figure 8.10 does not tell you what levels of a categorical variable are being compared. It tells you how the categorical variable is being transformed so that deviation contrasts for the parameter estimates are obtained. The appendix provides detailed information about all of the available contrasts.

Figure 8.11   Categorical variables with deviation coefficients

Variables in the Equation

	B	S.E.	Wald	df	Sig.	Exp(B)
AGE	-.052	.063	.686	1	.407	.949
CATACID			3.836	2	.147	
CATACID(1)	-.975	.641	2.312	1	.128	.377
CATACID(2)	-.059	.573	.011	1	.918	.943
XRAY	2.035	.837	5.903	1	.015	7.650
GRADE	.808	.823	.962	1	.327	2.243
STAGE	1.457	.768	3.597	1	.058	4.293
Constant	.736	3.735	.039	1	.844	2.088

Different coding schemes result in different logistic regression coefficients, but not in different conclusions. That is, even though the actual values of the coefficients differ between Figure 8.8 and Figure 8.11, they tell you the same thing. Figure 8.8 tells you the effect of category 1 compared to category 3, while Figure 8.11 tells you the effect of category 1 compared to the average effect of all of the categories. You can select the coding scheme to match the type of comparisons you want to make.

Interaction Terms

Just as in linear regression, you can include terms in the model that are products of single terms. For example, if it made sense, you could include a term for the *acid* by *age* interaction in your model. Interaction terms for categorical variables can also be computed. They are created as products of the values of the new variables. The stepwise variable selection methods treat interactions just as any other variables. This may lead to models that contain interactions without the corresponding main effects. Such models may be difficult to interpret.

Selecting Predictor Variables

In logistic regression, as in other multivariate statistical techniques, you may want to identify subsets of independent variables that are good predictors of the dependent variable. All of the problems associated with variable selection algorithms in regression and discriminant analysis are found in logistic regression as well. None of the algorithms result in a "best" model in any statistical sense. Different algorithms for variable selection may result in different models. It is a good idea to examine several possible models and choose from among them on the basis of interpretability, parsimony, and ease of variable acquisition.

As always, the model is selected to fit a particular sample well, so there is no assurance that the same model will be selected if another sample from the same population is taken. The model will almost always fit the sample better than the population from which it is selected.

The SPSS Logistic Regression procedure has several methods available for model selection. You can enter variables into the model at will. You can also use forward stepwise selection and backward stepwise elimination for automated model building. The score statistic is always used for entering variables into a model. The Wald statistic, the change in likelihood, or the conditional statistic can be used for removing variables from a model (Lawless and Singhal, 1978). All variables that are used to represent the same categorical variable are entered or removed from the model together.

Forward Stepwise Selection

Forward stepwise variable selection in logistic regression proceeds the same way as in multiple linear regression. You start out with a model that contains only the constant unless the option to omit the constant term from the model is selected. At each step, the variable with the smallest significance level for the score statistic, provided it is less than the chosen cutoff value (by default 0.05), is entered into the model. All variables in the forward stepwise block that have been entered are then examined to see if they meet removal criteria. If the Wald statistic is used for deleting variables, the Wald statistics for all variables in the model are examined and the variable with the largest significance level for the Wald statistic, provided it exceeds the chosen cutoff value (by default 0.1), is removed from the model. If no variables meet removal criteria, the next eligible variable is entered into the model.

If a variable is selected for removal and it results in a model that has already been considered, variable selection stops. Otherwise, the model is estimated without the deleted variable and the variables are again examined for removal. This continues until no more variables are eligible for removal. Then variables are again examined for entry into the model. The process continues until either a previously considered model is encountered (which means the algorithm is cycling) or no variables meet entry or removal criteria.

The Likelihood-Ratio Test

A better criterion than the Wald statistic for determining variables to be removed from the model is the **likelihood-ratio (LR) test**. This involves estimating the model with each variable eliminated in turn and looking at the change in −2 log-likelihood when each variable is deleted. If the null hypothesis is true and the sample size is sufficiently large, the change has a chi-square distribution with r degrees of freedom, where r is the difference between the number of terms in the full model and the reduced model.

When the likelihood-ratio test is used for removing terms from a model, its significance level is compared to the cutoff value. The algorithm proceeds as previously described but with the likelihood-ratio statistic, instead of the Wald statistic, being evaluated for removing variables.

You can also use the **conditional statistic** to test for removal. Like the likelihood-ratio test, the conditional statistic is based on the difference in the likelihood for the reduced and full models. However, the conditional statistic is computationally much less intensive since it does not require that the model be reestimated without each of the variables.

An Example of Forward Selection

To see what the output looks like for forward selection, consider Figure 8.12, which contains statistics for variables not in the equation when only the constant is included in the model.

Figure 8.12   Variables not in the equation

Variables not in the Equation

			Score	df	Sig.
Step 0	Variables	AGE	1.095	1	.295
		ACID	3.117	1	.077
		XRAY	11.283	1	.001
		STAGE	7.438	1	.006
		GRADE	4.074	1	.044
	Overall Statistics		19.451	5	.002

The last row of the table, labeled Overall Statistics, tests the null hypothesis that the coefficients for all variables not in the model are 0. (This statistic is calculated from the score statistics, so it is not exactly the same value as the improvement chi-square value that you see in Figure 8.7. In general, however, the two statistics should be similar in value.) If the observed significance level for the statistic is small (that is, if you have reason to reject the hypothesis that all of the coefficients are 0), it is sensible to proceed with variable selection. If you can't reject the hypothesis that the coefficients are 0, you should consider terminating variable selection. If you continue to build a model, there is a reasonable chance that your resulting model will not be useful for other samples from the same population.

In this example, the hypothesis that all coefficients are zero can be rejected, so we can proceed with variable selection. In Figure 8.12, for each variable not in the model, the score statistic and its significance level (if the variable were entered next into the model) are shown. The score statistic is an efficient alternative to the Wald statistic for testing the hypothesis that a coefficient is 0. Unlike the Wald statistic, it does not require the explicit computation of parameter estimates, so it is useful in situations where recalculating parameter estimates for many different models would be computationally prohibitive. The likelihood-ratio statistic, the Wald statistic, and Rao's efficient score statistic are all equivalent in large samples, when the null hypothesis is true (Rao, 1973).

Figure 8.13   Coefficients for variables

Variables in the Equation

		B	S.E.	Wald	df	Sig.	Exp(B)
Step 1[1]	XRAY	2.182	.697	9.783	1	.002	8.861
	Constant	-1.170	.382	9.403	1	.002	.310
Step 2[2]	XRAY	2.119	.747	8.054	1	.005	8.326
	STAGE	1.588	.700	5.148	1	.023	4.895
	Constant	-2.045	.610	11.236	1	.001	.129

1. Variable(s) entered on step 1: XRAY.
2. Variable(s) entered on step 2: STAGE.

Figure 8.14   Statistics for variables not in the model

Variables not in the Equation

			Score	df	Sig.
Step 1	Variables	AGE	1.352	1	.245
		ACID	2.073	1	.150
		STAGE	5.639	1	.018
		GRADE	2.371	1	.124
	Overall Statistics		10.360	4	.035
Step 2	Variables	AGE	1.268	1	.260
		ACID	3.092	1	.079
		GRADE	.584	1	.445
	Overall Statistics		5.422	3	.143

Figure 8.15   Model summary statistics

Model Summary

Step	-2 Log likelihood	Cox & Snell R Square	Nagelkerke R Square
1	59.001	.191	.260
2	53.353	.273	.372

From Figure 8.12, you see that *xray* has the smallest observed significance level less than 0.05, the default value for entry, so it is the first variable entered into the model. For each step, the coefficients and associated statistics are shown in Figure 8.13. Statistics for variables not in the model are shown in Figure 8.14.

From Figure 8.14, you see that after step 2, when *stage* was entered into the model containing *xray*, none of the remaining variables could be included in the model since their observed significance levels are all greater than 0.05, the default value for variable entry. None of the variables in the model are eligible for removal since their observed significance levels are less than 0.10, the default value for variable removal.

Model summary statistics at each step are shown in Figure 8.15. (To obtain −2 log-likelihood for the model with only a constant, you must select the iteration history option. For this example, it is 70.252.) You can use the −2LL values shown in Figure 8.15 to calculate the change in −2LL values shown in Figure 8.16. For example, at step 1, the chi-square value is the difference in −2LL between the constant-only model (70.252) and the model with the constant and *xray* (59.001).

Figure 8.16   Changes in −2 log-likelihood

Improvement of Goodness-of-Fit

		Chi-square	df	Sig.
Step 1	Model	11.251	1	.001
	Block	11.251	1	.001
	Step	11.251	1	.001
Step 2	Model	16.899	2	.000
	Block	16.899	2	.000
	Step	5.647	1	.017

At step 2, the model chi-square is the difference in −2LL between the constant-only model and the model that contains the constant, *xray* and *stage* (70.252 − 53.353 = 16.899). The step chi-square value is the change in −2LL when *stage* was added to a model containing the constant and *xray* (59.001 − 53.353 = 5.648).

Forward Selection with the Likelihood-Ratio Criterion

If you select the likelihood-ratio statistic for deleting variables, the output will look slightly different from that previously described. For variables in the equation at a particular step, output similar to that shown in Figure 8.17 is produced in addition to the usual coefficients and Wald statistics.

Figure 8.17   Removal statistics

Model if Term Removed

Variable		Model Log Likelihood	Change in -2 Log Likelihood	df	Sig. of the Change
Step 1	XRAY	-35.126	11.251	1	.001
Step 2	XRAY	-31.276	9.199	1	.002
	STAGE	-29.500	5.647	1	.017

For each variable in the model, Figure 8.17 contains the log-likelihood for the model if the variable is removed from the model, the change in $-2LL$ if the variable is removed, as well as the observed significance level for the change. If the observed significance level is greater than the cutoff value for remaining in the model, the term is removed from the model and the model statistics are recalculated to see if any other variables are eligible for removal.

Backward Stepwise Elimination

Forward selection starts without any variables in the model. Backward elimination starts with all of the variables in the model. Then, at each step, variables are evaluated for entry and removal. The score statistic is always used for determining whether variables should be added to the model. Just as in forward selection, the Wald statistic, the likelihood-ratio statistic, or the conditional statistic can be used to select variables for removal.

Diagnostic Methods

Whenever you build a statistical model, it is important to examine the adequacy of the resulting model. In linear regression, we look at a variety of residuals, measures of influence, and indicators of collinearity. These are valuable tools for identifying points for which the model does not fit well, points that exert a strong influence on the coefficient estimates, and variables that are highly related to each other.

In logistic regression, there are comparable diagnostics that should be used to look for problems. However, in logistic regression, the evaluation of diagnostics is more complicated than in linear regression. The diagnostics should be calculated for each covariate pattern (combination of values of the independent variables). Unless there are adequate numbers of cases with the same covariate patterns, the diagnostic statistics may be difficult to interpret. (See Hosmer and Lemeshow, 1989, for further discussion.) Additionally, the interpretation of some of the diagnostic statistics depends on the values of the estimated probabilities.

The **residual** is the difference between the observed probability of the event and the predicted probability of the event based on the model. For example, if we predict the probability of malignant nodes to be 0.80 for a man who has malignant nodes, the residual is $1 - 0.80 = 0.20$.

The **standardized residual** is the residual divided by an estimate of its standard deviation. In this case, it is

$$Z_i = \frac{\text{Residual}_i}{\sqrt{P_i(1 - P_i)}}$$ **Equation 8.18**

For each case, the standardized residual can also be considered a component of the chi-square Pearson statistic. If the sample size is large, the standardized residuals should be approximately normally distributed, with a mean of 0 and a standard deviation of 1.

For each case, the **deviance** is computed as

$$-2 \times \log(\text{predicted probability for the observed group})$$ **Equation 8.19**

The deviance is calculated by taking the square root of the above statistic and attaching a negative sign if the event did not occur for that case. For example, the deviance for a man without malignant nodes and a predicted probability of 0.8 for nonmalignant nodes is

$$\text{Deviance} = -\sqrt{-2\log(0.8)} = -0.668$$ **Equation 8.20**

Large values for deviance indicate that the model does not fit the case well. For large sample sizes, the deviance is approximately normally distributed.

The **Studentized residual** for a case is approximately the square root of the change in the model deviance if the case is excluded. Discrepancies between the deviance and the Studentized residual may identify unusual cases. Normal probability plots of the Studentized residuals may be useful.

The **logit residual** is the residual for the model if it is predicted in the logit scale. That is,

$$\text{Logit residual}_i = \frac{\text{residual}_i}{P_i(1 - P_i)}$$ **Equation 8.21**

The **leverage** in logistic regression is in many respects analogous to the leverage in least-squares regression. Leverage values are often used for detecting observations that have a large impact on the predicted values. Unlike linear regression, the leverage values in logistic regression depend on both the dependent variable scores and the design matrix. Leverage values are bounded by 0 and 1. Their average value is p/n, where p is the number of estimated parameters in the model, including the constant, and n is the sample size. For cases with predicted probabilities less than 0.1 or greater than 0.9, the leverage values may be small even when the cases are influential.

Cook's distance is a measure of the influence of a case. It tells you how much deleting a case affects not only the residual for that case, but also the residuals of the remaining cases. Cook's distance (D) depends on the standardized residual for a case, as well as its leverage. It is defined as

$$D_i = \frac{Z_i^2 \times h_i}{(1 - h_i)}$$ Equation 8.22

where Z_i is the standardized residual and h_i is the leverage.

Another useful diagnostic measure is the change in the logistic coefficients when a case is deleted from the model, or **DfBeta**. You can compute this change for each coefficient, including the constant. For example, the change in the first coefficient when case i is deleted is

$$\text{DfBeta}(B_1^{(i)}) = B_1 - B_1^{(i)}$$ Equation 8.23

where B_1 is the value of the coefficient when all cases are included and $B_1^{(i)}$ is the value of the coefficient when the ith case is excluded. Large values for change identify observations that should be examined. The DfBeta values calculated by the logistic regression program are an approximation to the true values.

Plotting Diagnostics

All of the diagnostic statistics described in this chapter can be saved for further analysis. If you save the values for the diagnostics, you can, when appropriate, obtain normal probability plots using the Examine procedure and plot the diagnostics using the Graph procedure (see the *SPSS Base User's Guide* for more information on these procedures).

Figure 8.18 shows a normal probability plot and a detrended normal probability plot of the deviances. As you can see, the deviances do not appear to be normally distributed. That's because there are cases for which the model just doesn't fit well. In Figure 8.4, you see cases that have high probabilities for being in the incorrect group.

Figure 8.18   Normal probability of the deviances

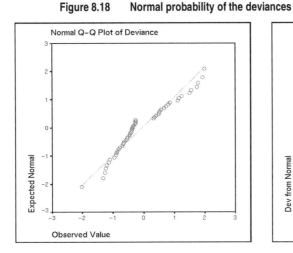

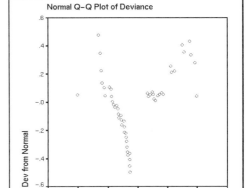

A plot of the standardized residuals against the case sequence numbers is shown in Figure 8.19. Again, you see cases with large values for the standardized residuals. Figure 8.20 shows that there is one case with a leverage value that is much larger than the rest. Similarly, Figure 8.21 shows that there is a case that has substantial impact on the estimation of the coefficient for *acid* (case 24). Examination of the data reveals that this case has the largest value for serum acid phosphatase and yet does not have malignant nodes. Since serum acid phosphatase was positively related to malignant nodes, as shown in Figure 8.2, this case is quite unusual. If we remove case 24 from the analysis, the coefficient for serum acid phosphatase changes from 0.0243 to 0.0490. A variable that was, at best, a very marginal predictor becomes much more important.

Figure 8.19   Plot of standardized residual with case ID

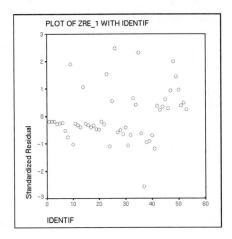

Figure 8.20   Plot of leverage with case ID

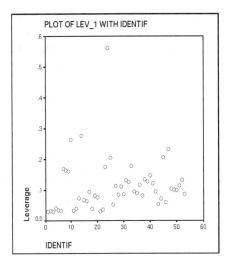

Figure 8.21   Plot of change in acid coefficient with case ID

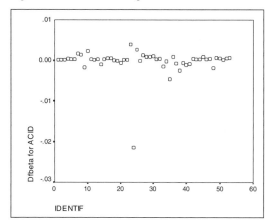

Another Look at Model Fit

Model Discrimination

In "Assessing the Goodness of Fit of the Model" on p. 42, two criteria for model evaluation were introduced: model discrimination and model calibration. Let's first consider model discrimination. Model discrimination tells you how well the model is able to distinguish between cases in the two groups. A perfect model always assigns higher probabilities to cases with the outcome of interest than to cases without the outcome of interest. In other words, the two sets of probabilities do not overlap.

A frequently used measure of the ability of a model to discriminate between the two groups of cases is the c statistic. The **c statistic** can be interpreted as the proportion of pairs of cases with different observed outcomes in which the model results in a higher probability for the cases with the event than for the case without the event. (The c statistic is equal to the area under the ROC curve. For further information, see Hanley and McNeil, 1982.) The c statistic ranges in value from 0.5 to 1. A value of 0.5 means that the model is no better than flipping a coin for assigning cases to groups. A value of 1 means that the model always assigns higher probabilities to cases with the event than to cases without the event.

To calculate the c statistic in SPSS, you must save the predicted probabilities from the logistic regression procedure. Then, you can use the ROC facility to calculate the area under the ROC curve. For the logistic regression model with all of the independent variables, the c statistic, from Figure 8.22, is 0.845. This means that in almost 85% of all possible pairs of cases in which one case has positive nodes and the other does not, the logistic regression model assigns a higher probability of having positive nodes to the case with positive nodes.

Figure 8.22   Area under the ROC curve

Area Under the Curve

Test Result Variable(s): Predicted probability

Area	Std. Error [1]	Asymptotic Sig. [2]	Asymptotic 95% Confidence Interval	
			Lower Bound	Upper Bound
.845	.054	.000	.740	.951

1. Under the nonparametric assumption
2. Null hypothesis: true area = 0.5

Model Calibration

Model calibration tells you how closely the observed and predicted probabilities match. A commonly used test for the goodness of fit of the observed and predicted number of events is the Hosmer and Lemeshow test. (Hosmer and Lemeshow, 1989). It is most useful when the number of covariate patterns is large and the standard goodness-of-fit chi-square tests cannot be used. To calculate the test, you divide the cases into 10 approximately equal groups based on the estimated probability of the event occurring (deciles of risk) and see how the observed and expected numbers of events and non-events compare. The chi-square test is used to assess the difference between the observed and expected numbers of events. To use this technique sensibly you must have a fairly large sample size so that the expected number of events in most groups exceeds 5 and none of the groups have expected values less than 1. Since the prostate data set is too small for the test to be useful, we'll consider survival data from 1085 patients hospitalized for septicemia, a life-threatening infection of the blood stream.[1]

---

1. Thanks to Michael Pine of Michael Pine and Associates for allowing use of these data.

Figure 8.23   Hosmer-Lemeshow table

Contingency Table for Hosmer and Lemeshow Test

	DEAD = .00		DEAD = 1.00		
	Observed	Expected	Observed	Expected	Total
1	103	103.471	2	1.529	105
2	103	105.532	6	3.468	109
3	103	103.893	6	5.107	109
4	109	109.991	10	9.009	119
5	90	87.575	8	10.425	98
6	94	96.363	17	14.637	111
7	97	90.847	12	18.153	109
8	84	85.830	26	24.170	110
9	79	73.717	30	35.283	109
10	36	40.781	70	65.219	106

Figure 8.23 shows the table upon which the Hosmer and Lemeshow goodness-of-fit test is based for a logistic regression model that predicts death from septicemia. The cases are divided into 10 approximately equal groups, based on the values for the predicted probability of death. The number of cases in each group is shown in the *Total* column. The groups are not exactly equal since cases with the same combination of values for the independent variables are kept in the same group. For each group, the observed and predicted number of deaths and the observed and predicted number of survivors are shown. For example, in the first group of 105 cases, 2 died and 103 survived. Summing the predicted probabilities of death for these 105 cases, the predicted number of deaths is 1.53 and the predicted number of survivors is 103.47.

   To calculate the Hosmer and Lemeshow goodness-of-fit chi-square, you compute the difference between the observed and predicted number of cases in each of the cells. You then calculate $(O-E)^2/E$ for each of the cells in the table. The chi-square value is the sum of this quantity over all of the cells. For this example, the chi-square value is 8.17 with 8 degrees of freedom, as shown in Figure 8.24. (The degrees of freedom are calculated as the number of groups minus 2). The observed significance level for the chi-square value is 0.42, so you do not reject the null hypothesis that there is no difference between the observed and predicted values. The model appears to fit the data reasonably well.

   The value for the Hosmer and Lemeshow statistic depends on how the cases are grouped. (That's why different software packages may give different values for the same data set.) If there is a small number of groups, the test will usually indicate that the model fits, even if it does not. If you have a very large number of cases, the value of the

Hosmer and Lemeshow statistic can be large, even if the model fits well, since the value of a chi-square statistic is proportional to sample size. In summary, the Hosmer and Lemeshow statistic provides useful information about the calibration of the model, but it must be interpreted with care.

Figure 8.24   Hosmer-Lemeshow chi-square

Hosmer and Lemeshow Test

Step	Chi-square	df	Sig.
1	8.171	8	.417

9

Multinomial Logistic Regression Examples

When you have a dependent variable that is **binary**—it can have only two values—you can use binary logistic regression to model the relationship between the dependent variable and a set of independent variables. For example, you can model the probability that someone will buy your product based on characteristics such as age, education, gender, and income. See Chapter 8 for further discussion of two-group logistic regression.

If you have a categorical dependent variable with more than two possible values, you can use an extension of the binary logistic regression model, called **multinomial** or **polytomous logistic regression**, to examine the relationship between the dependent variable and a set of predictor variables. The models are called multinomial since for each combination of values (or covariate pattern) of the independent variables, the counts of the dependent variable are assumed to have a multinomial distribution. The counts at the different combinations are also assumed to be independent with a fixed total. You can use multinomial logistic regression to study the relationship between marital status and socioeconomic and psychological measures. If your dependent variable is ordinal (such as severe, moderate, and minimal), special types of logistic regression models may be useful (see Agresti, 1990).

SPSS has two procedures that can be used to build logistic regression models: the Binary Logistic Regression procedure and the Multinomial Logistic Regression procedure. Both procedures can be used to build binary regression models. See Chapter 1 for a discussion of differences between the two procedures. The SPSS Multinomial Logistic Regression procedure described in this chapter can also be used to analyze data from one-on-one matched case-control studies. These are studies that construct matched pairs of cases—one has experienced the event of interest, the other has not. Case-control studies are often used in medicine to identify predictors of the event. Matched case-control studies are discussed in more detail on p. 78.

The Logit Model

When you have two groups, one that has experienced the event of interest and the other that has not, you can write the logistic regression model as

$$\log\left(\frac{P(event)}{1 - P(event)}\right) = B_0 + B_1 X_1 + B_2 X_2 + \ldots + B_p X_p$$

where B_0 is the intercept, B_1 to B_p are the logistic regression coefficients, and X_1 to X_p are the independent variables. The quantity on the left side of the equals sign is called a **logit**. It is the natural log of the odds that the event will occur. When the dependent variable has only two values, there is only one nonredundant logit that can be formed. That is because modeling the logit $\log((1 - P(event))/P(event))$ would result in the same logistic regression coefficients for the independent variables, but the signs would be reversed.

If your dependent variable has J possible values, the number of nonredundant logits you can form is $J - 1$. The simplest type of logit for this situation is called the **baseline category logit**. It compares each category to a baseline category. See Agresti (1990) for discussion of logit types when the dependent variable is ordinal. If the baseline category is J, for the ith category, the model is

$$\log\left(\frac{P(category_i)}{P(category_J)}\right) = B_{i0} + B_{i1} X_1 + B_{i2} X_2 + \ldots + B_{ip} X_p$$

You will have a set of coefficients for each logit. That's why each coefficient has two subscripts: the first identifies the logit and the second identifies the variable. For the baseline category, the coefficients are all 0. For example, if the dependent variable has three values, you will generate two sets of nonzero coefficients, one for the comparison of each of the first two groups to the last group.

Baseline Logit Example

As an example of multinomial logistic regression, we'll look at the 1992 presidential race. The 1996 General Social Survey asked people whom they voted for in 1992. This data set can be found in *voter.sav*.

From the menus choose:

Analyze
  Descriptive Statistics
    Crosstabs...

▸ Row(s): sex

▸ Column(s): pres92

Cells
  Percentages
    ☑ Row

Figure 9.1   Crosstabulation of the responses by gender

RESPONDENTS SEX * VOTE FOR CLINTON, BUSH, PEROT Crosstabulation

			VOTE FOR CLINTON, BUSH, PEROT			
			Bush	Perot	Clinton	Total
RESPONDENTS SEX	male	Count	315	152	337	804
		% within RESPONDENTS SEX	39.2%	18.9%	41.9%	100.0%
	female	Count	346	126	571	1043
		% within RESPONDENTS SEX	33.2%	12.1%	54.7%	100.0%
Total		Count	661	278	908	1847
		% within RESPONDENTS SEX	35.8%	15.1%	49.2%	100.0%

Figure 9.1 is a crosstabulation of the responses by gender. From the row percentages, you see that 42% of the men and 55% of the women voted for Clinton. Let's consider a simple multinomial logistic regression model to study the relationship between presidential choice and gender.

Since the dependent variable has three categories, two nonredundant logits can be formed using Clinton as the base or reference category and gender as the single independent variable:

$$g_1 = \log\left(\frac{P(\text{Bush})}{P(\text{Clinton})}\right) = B_{10} + B_{11}(male)$$

$$g_2 = \log\left(\frac{P(\text{Perot})}{P(\text{Clinton})}\right) = B_{20} + B_{21}(male)$$

The gender variable has two values, so we arbitrarily select *female* as the reference category and set the coefficients for females to 0. The SPSS Multinomial Logistic Regression procedure treats the last category of a categorical or factor variable as the reference category. In the General Social Survey, males are coded with 1 and females are coded with 2, so *female* is the reference category.

Parameter Estimates

From the menus choose:

Analyze
  Regression
    Multinomial Logistic...

▶ Dependent: pres92

▶ Factor(s): sex

Statistics
  ☐ Summary statistics (deselect)
  ☐ Likelihood ratio test (deselect)
  ☑ Parameter estimates (default)
  Confidence interval: 95% (default)

Figure 9.2   Parameter estimates for model with intercept and gender

Parameter Estimates

VOTE FOR CLINTON, BUSH, PEROT		B	Std. Error	Wald	df	Sig.	Exp(B)	95% Confidence Interval for Exp(B)	
								Lower Bound	Upper Bound
Bush	Intercept	-.501	.068	54.067	1	.000			
	[SEX=1]	.433	.104	17.422	1	.000	1.543	1.258	1.891
	[SEX=2]	0ᵃ	0	.	0	.	.	.	.
Perot	Intercept	-1.511	.098	235.703	1	.000			
	[SEX=1]	.715	.139	26.572	1	.000	2.044	1.558	2.682
	[SEX=2]	0ᵃ	0	.	0	.	.	.	.

a. This parameter is set to 0 because it is redundant.

The two sets of logistic regression coefficients are shown in Figure 9.2. Using these co-efficients, the logit equations can be written as

$$g_1 = \log\left(\frac{P(\text{Bush})}{P(\text{Clinton})}\right) = -0.50 + 0.433(male)$$

$$g_2 = \log\left(\frac{P(\text{Perot})}{P(\text{Clinton})}\right) = -1.51 + 0.715(male)$$

where *male* is 1 for men, 0 for women.

   The intercept terms are simply the logits for females. For example, the first intercept is the log of the ratio of the probability of a female choosing Bush to the probability of a female choosing Clinton, or $\log(346/571)$. The second intercept is the log of the ratio of the probability of a female choosing Perot to the probability of a female choosing Clinton. The coefficients for male tell you about the relationship between the logits and gender. Since both coefficients are positive and significantly different from 0, you know that males are more likely than females to select both Bush and Perot as compared to Clinton. In fact, as you can see from the column labeled *Exp(B)*, a male is 1.54 times more likely than a female to choose Bush than Clinton, and 2.04 times more likely than a female to choose Perot than Clinton. See "Interpreting the Regression Coefficients" on p. 40 in Chapter 8 for a more detailed discussion.

Obtaining the Third Pairwise Comparison

The coefficients in Figure 9.2 describe the relationship between gender and the two logits, with Clinton as the reference category. However, there is an additional pairwise comparison that you can make—Bush to Perot. Since this is a redundant logit, you can obtain the coefficients for this comparison as the difference of the two sets of coefficients you have already estimated. That's because

$$\log\left(\frac{P(\text{Bush})}{P(\text{Perot})}\right) = \log\left(\frac{P(\text{Bush})}{P(\text{Clinton})}\right) - \log\left(\frac{P(\text{Perot})}{P(\text{Clinton})}\right)$$

Remember that $\log(a/b) = \log(a) - \log(b)$. However, if you are interested in this logit, it may be simpler to just recode your data so that Perot is the last category, the reference category. The procedure will then automatically calculate the coefficients and standard errors of interest.

Adding Education to the Model

You have seen that the gender of the voter appears to be related to the candidate selected. Let's see whether years of education is also a significant predictor when it is added to a model that already contains gender.

Recall the Multinomial Logistic Regression dialog box and select:

▶ Factor(s): sex

▶ Covariate(s): educ

Figure 9.3   Parameter estimates for gender and years of education

Parameter Estimates

VOTE FOR CLINTON, BUSH, PEROT		B	Std. Error	Wald	df	Sig.	Exp(B)	95% Confidence Interval for Exp(B)	
								Lower Bound	Upper Bound
Bush	Intercept	-.702	.259	7.318	1	.007			
	EDUC	1.466E-02	.018	.656	1	.418	1.015	.979	1.051
	[SEX=1]	.428	.104	16.970	1	.000	1.535	1.252	1.881
	[SEX=2]	0ᵃ	0	.	0	.	.	.	.
Perot	Intercept	-1.894	.353	28.859	1	.000			
	EDUC	2.716E-02	.024	1.248	1	.264	1.028	.980	1.078
	[SEX=1]	.715	.139	26.396	1	.000	2.043	1.556	2.684
	[SEX=2]	0ᵃ	0	.	0	.	.	.	.

a. This parameter is set to 0 because it is redundant.

Figure 9.3 contains the parameter estimates for the model with gender and years of education. From this table, you see that including education has not changed the coefficients for gender. You also see that for both logits the coefficient for years of education is not significantly different from 0.

Does that mean that education is not an important predictor of voting choice? Not necessarily. It is certainly possible that education is related to candidate choice but not in a linear fashion. To test this, instead of entering the actual years of education into the model, let's consider highest degree achieved (0 = less than high school, 1= high school, 2 = junior college, 3 = bachelor's, and 4 = graduate degree).

Recall the Multinomial Logistic Regression dialog box and select:

▶ Factor(s): sex, degree

Figure 9.4   Parameter estimates for model with intercept, gender, and highest degree received

Parameter Estimates

VOTE FOR CLINTON BUSH, PEROT		B	Std. Error	Wald	df	Sig.	Exp(B)	95% Confidence Interval for Exp(B) Lower Bound	Upper Bound
Bush	Intercept	-.805	.168	22.879	1	.000			
	[SEX=1]	.458	.105	19.148	1	.000	1.581	1.288	1.941
	[SEX=2]	0ᵃ	0	.	0	.	.	.	.
	[DEGREE=0]	-.198	.228	.760	1	.383	.820	.525	1.281
	[DEGREE=1]	.387	.175	4.913	1	.027	1.473	1.046	2.074
	[DEGREE=2]	.431	.253	2.914	1	.088	1.539	.938	2.525
	[DEGREE=3]	.424	.195	4.745	1	.029	1.529	1.043	2.239
	[DEGREE=4]	0ᵃ	0	.	0	.	.	.	.
Perot	Intercept	-2.188	.264	68.527	1	.000			
	[SEX=1]	.760	.140	29.319	1	.000	2.139	1.624	2.816
	[SEX=2]	0ᵃ	0	.	0	.	.	.	.
	[DEGREE=0]	-.502	.393	1.627	1	.202	.605	.280	1.309
	[DEGREE=1]	.833	.267	9.709	1	.002	2.299	1.362	3.882
	[DEGREE=2]	1.052	.346	9.263	1	.002	2.864	1.454	5.640
	[DEGREE=3]	.804	.291	7.608	1	.006	2.233	1.262	3.953
	[DEGREE=4]	0ᵃ	0	.	0	.	.	.	.

a. This parameter is set to 0 because it is redundant.

From Figure 9.4, you see that the *degree* parameter estimates have an interesting pattern. The first parameter estimate represents people with less than a high school education compared to people with a graduate degree. For both of the logits, you cannot reject the null hypothesis that the coefficients are 0. That is, you don't have enough evidence to conclude that people with less than a high school education and those with graduate degrees voted differently. The next three coefficients represent people who graduated from high school but don't have graduate degrees. Within a logit, the three parameter estimates are fairly similar and all but one of them are significantly different from 0. It appears that these three groups behave similarly to each other but differently from those with a graduate degree. The relationship between highest degree earned and voting preference is nonlinear, with the highest and lowest education levels differing from those in the middle. This is not really a surprising finding. It has been noticed before that Democratic candidates are favored by both those with little formal education and those who have advanced degrees. It may make sense to replace the degree variable with a new binary variable that is coded 1 for less than high school or graduate degree and coded 0 otherwise.

Likelihood-Ratio Test

Recall the Multinomial Logistic Regression dialog box and select:

Statistics
    ☑ Likelihood ratio test
    ☐ Parameter estimates (deselect)

Figure 9.5   Likelihood-ratio tests for model with intercept, gender, and degree

Likelihood Ratio Tests

Effect	-2 Log Likelihood of Reduced Model	Chi-Square	df	Sig.
Intercept	103.601	.000	0	.
SEX	140.753	37.153	2	.000
DEGREE	144.590	40.990	8	.000

The chi-square statistic is the difference in -2 log-likelihoods between the final model and a reduced model. The reduced model is formed by omitting an effect from the final model. The null hypothesis is that all parameters of that effect are 0.

Figure 9.5 contains likelihood-ratio tests for the individual effects in the final model that includes gender and degree. The test for each effect is based on the change in the value of −2 log-likelihood if the effect is removed from the final model. If all coefficients for an effect are 0, this change has a chi-square distribution with degrees of freedom equal to the degrees of freedom for the effect being removed. From Figure 9.5, you can conclude that both gender and degree are significantly related to voting choice. The change in −2 log-likelihood is significant if sex is removed from the model containing the intercept, sex, and degree. There is also a significant change if degree is removed from the model containing the intercept, sex, and degree. The likelihood-ratio tests in Figure 9.5 provide better tests for an effect than those based on the Wald statistics shown in previous tables. That's because tests based on the Wald statistic sometimes fail to correctly reject the null hypothesis when coefficients are large. (See Hauck and Donner, 1977.) Notice also that the likelihood-ratio tests provide overall tests for the effects, while the Wald tests in Figure 9.4 are for each category within a logit. You can obtain tests for linear combinations of parameters using the TEST subcommand in syntax.

Recall the Multinomial Logistic Regression dialog box and select:

Statistics
    ☐ Likelihood ratio test (deselect)

Figure 9.6   Model fitting information

Model Fitting Information

Model	-2 Log Likelihood	Chi-Square	df	Sig.
Intercept Only	178.457			
Final	103.601	74.856	10	.000

From Figure 9.6, you can see the value of the −2 log-likelihood both for the model with only the intercept terms and for the final model. The difference between these values is shown in the column labeled *Chi-Square*. If the observed significance level is small, you can reject the null hypothesis that all coefficients for gender and degree are 0. You can conclude that the final model is significantly better than the intercept-only model. The log-likelihood can be expressed as the sum of a multinomial constant that doesn't depend on the parameters, and the kernel, a quantity that does depend on the parameters. The −2 log-likelihood values in Figure 9.6 include both the constant and the kernel. Many books and programs, including SPSS logistic regression, report only the kernel values. Since most tests are based on differences of log-likelihoods, the constants do not matter. If the number of cases is equal to the number of covariate patterns, the constant is 0.

So far, we have considered the effect of gender and highest degree earned on voting behavior. Both of these variables are significantly related to candidate preference. We've looked at the effects of the variables individually, but we have not considered a possible interaction between gender and highest degree. There is an interaction effect between gender and degree earned if the effect of degree is not the same for men and women. For example, it's possible that highly educated women favored Clinton even more than you would predict based only on the coefficients for gender and education.

Recall the Multinomial Logistic Regression dialog box and select:

Model
    ⊙ Full Factorial

Statistics
    ☑ Likelihood ratio test

Figure 9.7   Likelihood ratio tests for effects in the mode

Likelihood Ratio Tests

Effect	-2 Log Likelihood of Reduced Model	Chi-Square	df	Sig.
Intercept	97.227	.000	0	.
SEX	97.227	.000	0	.
DEGREE	97.227	.000	0	.
SEX * DEGREE	103.601	6.374	8	.605

The chi-square statistic is the difference in -2 log-likelihoods between the final model and a reduced model. The reduced model is formed by omitting an effect from the final model. The null hypothesis is that all parameters of that effect are 0.

From Figure 9.7, you see that when the sex-by-degree interaction is removed from the model, the change in –2 log-likelihood is not large enough to reject the null hypothesis that all of the coefficients associated with the interaction effect are 0. The intercept and main effects of sex and degree are included in the interaction and removing them doesn't change the fit of the model. The likelihood-ratio test is not calculated for these effects.

Calculating Predicted Probabilities and Expected Frequencies

From the logistic regression model coefficients, you can estimate the probability that a person will vote for each of the three candidates. As an example, let's calculate the probability that a man with a bachelor's degree votes for each of the candidates. First, you must estimate the values of each of the three logits, using the values for the intercept and the coefficients for male and bachelor's degree:

$$g_1 = -0.8046 + 0.4582 + 0.4244 = 0.0780$$
$$g_2 = -2.1883 + 0.7601 + 0.8035 = -0.6247$$
$$g_3 = 0$$

Remember that for the reference group (the last group), all coefficients are 0. Then, for each group calculate

$$P(group_i) = \frac{\exp(g_i)}{\sum_{k=1}^{J} \exp(g_k)}$$

The estimated probabilities for a male with a bachelor's degree are

$$P(\text{Bush}) = \frac{1.081}{(1 + 1.081 + 0.535)} = 0.413$$

$$P(\text{Perot}) = \frac{0.535}{(1 + 1.081 + 0.535)} = 0.205$$

$$P(\text{Clinton}) = \frac{1}{(1 + 1.081 + 0.535)} = 0.382$$

There are 160 men with bachelor's degree in our data set. Based on the estimated probabilities, you would predict that 66.1 voted for Bush, 32.8 voted for Perot, and 61.1 voted for Clinton.

Recall the Multinomial Logistic Regression dialog box and select:

Model
⊙ Main Effects

Statistics
☐ Likelihood ratio test (deselect)
☑ Cell Probabilities

Figure 9.8   Observed and predicted frequencies and residuals for a model with gender and degree

Observed and Predicted Frequencies

HIGHEST DEGREE	GENDER	VOTE FOR	Frequency			Percentage	
			Observed	Predicted	Pearson Residual	Observed	Predicted
bachelor	male	Bush	71	66.108	.785	44.4%	41.3%
		Perot	27	32.743	-1.125	16.9%	20.5%
		Clinton	62	61.149	.138	38.8%	38.2%

The percentages are based on total observed frequencies in each subpopulation.

Only the covariate pattern of males with bachelor degrees is shown in Figure 9.8, the table of observed and predicted frequencies (calculated more precisely). From Figure 9.8, you see that 71 men actually voted for Bush, 27 for Perot, and 62 for Clinton. For each cell, the Pearson residual is also calculated. The Pearson residual is the difference between the observed and predicted cell counts divided by an estimate of the standard deviation. The Pearson residuals are used to assess how well a model fits the observed data. Cells with Pearson residuals greater than 2 in absolute value should be examined to see if there is an identifiable reason why the model does not fit well. None of the residuals in Figure 9.8 are particularly large.

Classification Table

If you classify each case into the group for which it has the highest predicted probability, you can compare the observed and predicted groups.

Recall the Multinomial Logistic Regression dialog box and select:

Statistics
☐ Cell Probabilities (deselect)
☑ Classification Table

Figure 9.9   Classification table

Classification

Observed	Predicted			
	Bush	Perot	Clinton	Percent Correct
Bush	251	0	410	38.0%
Perot	133	0	145	.0%
Clinton	237	0	671	73.9%
Overall Percentage	33.6%	.0%	66.4%	49.9%

From Figure 9.9, you see that of the 661 people who actually voted for Bush, 251 are correctly assigned to Bush by the model. Only 38% of Bush supporters are correctly classified. None of the Perot voters are correctly classified. Almost three-quarters of the Clinton voters are correctly identified. Overall, about half of the voters are correctly assigned. Does this mean the model doesn't fit? Not necessarily. It is possible for the model to be correct but classification to be poor. When you have groups of unequal sizes, as in this example, cases will be more likely to be classified to the larger groups, regardless of how well the model fits. Although a classification table provides interesting information, by itself it tells you little about how well a model fits the data. (See Hosmer and Lemeshow, 1989, for further discussion.)

Goodness-of-Fit Tests

Whenever you build a model, you are interested in knowing how well it fits the observed data. The Pearson chi-square statistic is often used to assess the discrepancy between observed and expected counts in a multidimensional crosstabulation. It is computed in the usual manner as

$$\chi^2_{Pearson} = \sum_{all\ cells} \frac{(\text{observed count} - \text{expected count})^2}{\text{expected count}}$$

Large values for the Pearson χ^2 indicate that the model does not fit well. If the observed significance level is small, you can reject the null hypothesis that your model fits the observed data. Another measure of goodness of fit is the deviance chi-square. It is the change in –2 log-likelihood when the model is compared to a *saturated* model—that is, when it is compared to a model that has all main effects and interactions. If the model fits well, the difference between the log-likelihoods should be small, and the observed significance level should be large. For large sample sizes, both goodness-of-fit statistics should be similar.

The degrees of freedom for both statistics depend on the number of distinct observed combinations of the independent variables (often called the number of covariate patterns), the number of independent logits, and the number of parameters estimated. In this example, the two independent variables form 10 cells, all of them with observed counts greater than 0; the number of independent logits is 2; and the number of estimated parameters is 12. The degrees of freedom are the product of the number of observed covariate patterns and the number of independent logits, minus the number of estimated parameters. The degrees of freedom are $(10 \times 2) - 12 = 8$.

Recall the Multinomial Logistic Regression dialog box and select:

Statistics
    ☐ Classification Table (deselect)
    ☑ Goodness of fit chi-square statistics

Figure 9.10   Goodness-of-fit statistics for a model with gender and degree

Goodness-of-Fit

	Chi-Square	df	Sig.
Pearson	6.327	8	.611
Deviance	6.374	8	.605

From Figure 9.10, you see that you cannot reject the null hypothesis that the model fits. Notice that the deviance chi-square in Figure 9.10 is the same as the likelihood-ratio chi-square for the sex-by-degree interaction in Figure 9.7. That's not a coincidence. The saturated model for Figure 9.10 is the model with sex, degree, and the sex-by-degree interaction. In both Figure 9.10 and Figure 9.7, you are looking at the change in –2 log-likelihood when the interaction is removed from the saturated model.

The goodness-of-fit statistics should be used only when there are multiple cases observed for each of the covariate patterns. If most cases have unique covariate patterns, as is often the situation when covariates are not categorical, the goodness-of-fit tests will not have a chi-square distribution, since the expected values for the cells will be small. (See Hosmer and Lemeshow, 1989.)

Another consideration when evaluating the goodness of fit of a model is determining whether to base the goodness-of-fit tests only on covariate patterns defined by variables in the model or to include additional variables that define the table. For example, if voters were cross-classified on the basis of gender, age group, and degree but if the final model included only gender and degree, the values of the goodness-of-fit tests would differ, depending on whether the covariate patterns were combinations of only degree and gender or whether the covariate patterns were combinations of degree, gender, and age group. That's because the saturated models are different in the two situations. The SPSS Multinomial Logistic Regression procedure allows you to specify the variables to be used for the saturated model by specifying them on the subpopulation subcommand. This feature also allows you to calculate the change in –2 log-likelihood when a set of variables is removed from a model. (See Simonoff, 1998, for further discussion.)

Examining the Residuals

As in other statistical procedures, the examination of residuals and other diagnostic statistics plays an important role in the evaluation of the suitability of a particular model. In this release of SPSS, the Multinomial Logistic Regression procedure does not save any diagnostics or provide any diagnostic plots. For certain models, you can use the Logit or Logistic Regression procedure to calculate and examine diagnostic measures.

Pseudo R^2 Measures

In linear models, the R^2 statistic represents the proportion of variability in the dependent variable that can be explained by the independent variables. It is easily calculated and interpreted. For logistic regression models, an easily interpretable measure of the strength of the relationship between the dependent variable and the independent variables is not available, although a variety of measures have been proposed.

Recall the Multinomial Logistic Regression dialog box and select:

Statistics
   ☑ Summary statistics
   ☐ Goodness of fit chi-square statistics (deselect)

Figure 9.11   Pseudo R-square statistics

Pseudo R-Square

Cox and Snell	.040
Nagelkerke	.046
McFadden	.020

SPSS calculates three such pseudo R^2 statistics, as shown in Figure 9.11. The first two are discussed in Chapter 8. McFadden's R^2 is calculated as

$$R^2_{McFadden} = \frac{l(0) - l(B)}{l(0)}$$

where $l(B)$ is the kernel of the log-likelihood of the model, and $l(0)$ is the kernel of the log-likelihood of the intercept-only model. McFadden's R^2 is the proportion of the kernel of the log-likelihood explained by the logistic regression model.

Correcting for Overdispersion

Most statistical procedures for categorical data assume what is called multinomial sampling. However, the parameter estimates obtained from most procedures are the same for sampling under other models, such as the Poisson. Occasionally, data show more variability than you would expect based on the sampling scheme. This is called **overdispersion**. Different causes such as correlated observations or mixtures of different distributions can result in overdispersion. It is possible to estimate constants from the data that you can use to correct the variance-covariance matrix of parameter estimates. (See McCullagh and Nelder, 1989.) The Multinomial Logistic Regression procedure can estimate correction factors for overdispersion. The Wald tests are then based on the corrected values.

Matched Case-Control Studies

Logistic regression models can be used to analyze data from several different experimental designs. For example, you can take a single random sample of people and then determine who experienced the event of interest (cases) and who did not (controls), or you can take two independent samples, one of cases and one of controls. Sampling cases and controls separately is particularly useful for rare events because you can be sure that you will have enough events to analyze. For both of these situations, the coefficients for the independent variables from the usual logistic regression analysis procedures will be correct. However, for the two-sample situation, you will not be able to estimate the probability of the event in the population for various combinations of risk factors unless you know the sampling fractions for the cases and for the controls and adjust the intercept parameter accordingly. (See Hosmer and Lemeshow, 1989.)

Another type of experimental design that can be analyzed with logistic regression is the matched case-control study. In a matched case-control study, each case is paired with one or more controls that have the same values for preselected risk factors (matched factors), such as age or gender. For each case and control, information is also gathered about other possible risk factors (unmatched variables). The advantage of such a design is that differences between cases and controls with respect to an event can then be attributed to the unmatched risk factors. The SPSS Multinomial Logistic Regression procedure can be used to analyze data from matched case-control studies in which each case is paired with a single control. These are sometimes called **1–1 matched case-control studies**.

The Model

Consider a 1–1 matched design in which there are K matched pairs of cases and controls. The risk of an individual experiencing the event has two components: the risk associated with the matched variables and the risk associated with the unmatched variables. For a particular individual, the logit for experiencing the event can be written as

$$\log(\text{odds of event}) = \alpha_k + \sum_{i=1}^{p} B_i X_i$$

where α_k is the risk for the kth pair based on the values of the matched variables, X_1 to X_p are the values of the unmatched independent variables, and B_i is the logistic regression coefficient for the ith unmatched independent variable.

The log of the ratio of the odds that a case will experience the event to the odds that the corresponding control will experience the event can be written as

$$\log\left(\frac{\text{odds of event for case}}{\text{odds of event for control}}\right) = \sum_{i=1}^{p} B_i D_i$$

where B_i is the coefficient for the ith nonmatched independent variable, and D_i is the difference in values between the case and its matched control. The logistic regression coefficients are interpreted the same for matched and unmatched logistic regression analyses.

Creating the Difference Variables

The SPSS Multinomial Logistic Regression procedure can be used to analyze data from 1–1 matched designs, but the data file must be structured in a special way to reflect the pairing. For the paired analysis, the number of cases must be equal to the number of matched pairs, and the variables must be the differences in values between the case and the control. As an example, consider data from Appendix 3 of Hosmer and Lemeshow (1989). These data are available at *http://www-unix.oit.umass.edu/~statdata/data/ plowbwt.dat*, (copyright © John Wiley & Sons, Inc.). There are 56 pairs of mothers— one from each pair gave birth to a low-birth-weight baby, and the other did not. The women are matched on age. The variables we will consider are *lwt*, which is the last weight prior to pregnancy; *age*; *race* (1 = *white*, 2 = *black*, 3 = *other*); *smoke* (smoking during pregnancy, 0 = *no*, 1 = *yes*); *ptd* (previous preterm delivery, 0 = *no*, 1 = *yes*); and *ui* (uterine irritability, 0 = *no*, 1 = *yes*).

Figure 9.12   Data values and differences for a case control pair

	LOW	LWT	AGE	RACE	SMOKE	PTD	UI	RACE1	RACE2
Case	1	101	14	3	1	1	0	0	1
Control	0	135	14	1	0	0	0	0	0
Difference		−34		X	1	1	0	0	1

Figure 9.12 shows the data values and differences for one of the matched pairs. Although it seems easy to compute differences, categorical variables with more than two values pose some difficulties. Recall that for many statistical analyses categorical variables must be transformed prior to analysis (see "Categorical Variables" on p. 47 in Chapter 8). The SPSS Binary Logistic Regression and Multinomial Logistic Regression procedures automatically perform the transformation for variables identified as categorical. These variables must be identified as *factors* in the Multinomial Logistic Regression procedure or *categorical* in the Binary Logistic Regression procedure. However, to run a matched case-control analysis, you must create the new variables used to represent a categorical variable and find the differences between these new variables.

Figure 9.13   Indicator coding of RACE

	RACE1	RACE2
White	0	0
Black	1	0
Other	0	1

Consider a simple example. *Race* is a categorical variable with three values, so you will need two variables to represent it. If you use indicator coding with 1 (white) as the reference category, you must create two new variables, say *race1* and *race2*. *Race1* will be coded 1 for blacks; 0, otherwise. *Race2* will be coded 1 for others; 0, otherwise. Figure 9.13 shows the representation of the three race categories. For each case, you must compute the values of *race1* and *race2*. Then, for each case-control pair, you must calculate the difference between *race1* and *race2*, as shown in Figure 9.12, and use these new variables in the analysis. The same procedure must be followed for interaction terms. Interaction variables must be created first and then differenced.

To analyze a matched case-control study in SPSS Multinomial Logistic Regression, you will need a data file in which each observation consists of the differences for the unmatched variables between a case and the corresponding control. You may want to also keep the values for the matched variables on the record so that you can use them in interaction terms. The dependent variable must be set to a constant for all observations, and all of the difference variables must be identified as *covariates*. The intercept must also be suppressed. Matched variables cannot be entered into the model as main effects, since their difference values are 0 for all cases. However, matched variables in their un-differenced form can be included in interaction terms.

Examining the Results

Figure 9.14   Parameter estimates

Parameter Estimates

Low birth weight		B	Std. Error	Wald	df	Sig.	Exp(B)	95% Confidence Interval for Exp(B)	
								Lower Bound	Upper Bound
Yes	SMOKE	1.348	.568	5.631	1	.018	3.849	1.264	11.715
	UI	1.032	.664	2.418	1	.120	2.808	.764	10.316
	PTD	1.563	.706	4.897	1	.027	4.774	1.196	19.061
	RACE1	.861	.643	1.793	1	.181	2.365	.671	8.338
	RACE2	.469	.604	.603	1	.438	1.598	.489	5.219
	LWT	-9.29E-03	.009	1.051	1	.305	.991	.973	1.009

The parameter estimates for the case-control data set are shown in Figure 9.14. Although the original names of the variables are used, all of the variables represent differences between the case and control pairs.

Figure 9.15   Likelihood-ratio tests

Likelihood Ratio Tests

Effect	-2 Log Likelihood of Reduced Model	Chi-Square	df	Sig.
SMOKE	64.422	6.599	1	.010
UI	60.488	2.665	1	.103
PTD	64.030	6.207	1	.013
RACE1	59.680	1.857	1	.173
RACE2	58.440	.617	1	.432
LWT	58.970	1.147	1	.284

The chi-square statistic is the difference in -2 log-likelihoods between the final model and a reduced model. The reduced model is formed by omitting an effect from the final model. The null hypothesis is that all parameters of that effect are 0.

The likelihood-ratio tests for each of the effects are shown in Figure 9.15. The coefficients for all of the variables except last weight are positive. Only smoking and prior preterm delivery are significantly associated with the low-birth-weight outcome. Smoking increases the odds of low birth weight by a factor of 3.8; prior preterm delivery increases the odds of low birth weight by a factor of 4.8. These factors are found in the column labeled *Exp(B)* in Figure 9.14.

Figure 9.16   Model fitting summary

Model Fitting Information

Model	-2 Log Likelihood	Chi-Square	df	Sig.
Null	77.632			
Final	57.823	19.809	6	.003

From Figure 9.16, you can see that the independent variables are significantly associated with the outcome. The change in –2 log-likelihood is significant when the model with all of the variables is compared to the model with no independent variables and no intercept. You cannot use the goodness-of-fit tests to evaluate how well the model fits, since you don't have multiple observations at each combination of values of the differenced variables. All pairs have different combinations of values. Hosmer and Lemeshow (1989) present a detailed discussion of fitting models to these data, as well as assessing the fit of the model.

10 Probit Analysis Examples

How much insecticide does it take to kill a pest? How low does a sale price have to be to induce a consumer to buy a product? In both of these situations, we are concerned with evaluating the potency of a stimulus. In the first example, the stimulus is the amount of insecticide; in the second, it is the sale price of an object. The response we are interested in is all-or-none. An insect is either dead or alive; a sale is made or not. Since all insects and shoppers do not respond in the same way—that is, they have different tolerances for insecticides and sale prices—the problem must be formulated in terms of the proportion responding at each level of the stimulus.

Different mathematical models can be used to express the relationship between the proportion responding and the "dose" of one or more stimuli. In this chapter, we will consider two commonly used models: the probit response model and the logit response model. We will assume that we have one or more stimuli of interest and that each stimulus can have several doses. We expose different groups of individuals to the desired combinations of stimuli. For each combination, we record the number of individuals exposed and the number who respond.

Probit and Logit Response Models

In probit and logit models, instead of regressing the actual proportion responding on the values of the stimuli, we transform the proportion responding using either a logit or probit transformation. For a probit transformation, we replace each of the observed proportions with the value of the standard normal curve below which the observed proportion of the area is found.

For example, if half (0.5) of the subjects respond at a particular dose, the corresponding probit value is 0, since half of the area in a standard normal curve falls below a Z score of 0. If the observed proportion is 0.95, the corresponding probit value is 1.64.

If the logit transformation is used, the observed proportion P is replaced by

$$\ln\left(\frac{P}{1-P}\right)$$

Equation 10.1

83

This quantity is called a **logit**. If the observed proportion is 0.5, the logit-transformed value is 0, the same as the probit-transformed value. Similarly, if the observed proportion is 0.95, the logit-transformed value is 1.47. This differs somewhat from the corresponding probit value of 1.64. (In most situations, analyses based on logits and probits give very similar results.)

The regression model for the transformed response can be written as

$$\text{Transformed} P_i = A + BX_i \qquad \qquad \textbf{Equation 10.2}$$

where P_i is the observed proportion responding at dose X_i. (Usually, the log of the dose is used instead of the actual dose.) If there is more than one stimulus variable, terms are added to the model for each of the stimuli. The SPSS Probit Analysis procedure obtains maximum-likelihood estimates of the regression coefficients.

An Example

Finney (1971) presents data showing the effect of a series of doses of rotenone (an insecticide) when sprayed on *Macrosiphoniella sanborni*. Table 10.1 contains the concentration, the number of insects tested at each dose, the proportion dying, and the probit transformation of each of the observed proportions.

Table 10.1   Effects of rotenone

Dose	Number observed	Number dead	Proportion dead	Probit
10.2	50	44	0.88	1.18
7.7	49	42	0.86	1.08
5.1	46	24	0.52	0.05
3.8	48	16	0.33	-0.44
2.6	50	6	0.12	-1.18

Figure 10.1 is a plot of the observed probits against the logs of the concentrations. (On the menus, you specify *died* as the response frequency variable, *total* as the observation frequency variable, and *dose* as the covariate. You also ask for a log transformation of *dose*.) You can see that the relationship between the two variables is linear. If the relationship did not appear to be linear, the concentrations would have to be transformed in some other way in order to achieve linearity. If a suitable transformation could not be found, fitting a straight line would not be a reasonable strategy for modeling the data.

Figure 10.1   Plot of observed probits against logs of concentrations

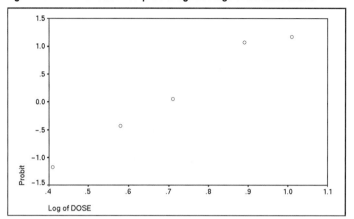

The parameter estimates and standard errors for this example are shown in Figure 10.2.

Figure 10.2   Parameter estimates and standard errors

```
Parameter estimates converged after 10 iterations.
Optimal solution found.

Parameter Estimates (PROBIT model:  (PROBIT(p)) = Intercept + BX):

           Regression Coeff.   Standard Error      Coeff./S.E.

 DOSE              4.16914             .47306          8.81306


                 Intercept   Standard Error   Intercept/S.E.

                 -2.85940           .34717         -8.23640

 Pearson  Goodness-of-Fit Chi Square =      1.621    DF = 3    P =  .655

 Since Goodness-of-Fit Chi square is NOT significant, no heterogeneity
 factor is used in the calculation of confidence limits.
```

The regression equation is

$$\text{Probit}(P_i) \ = \ -2.86 + 4.17(\log_{10}(\text{dose}_i)) \qquad\qquad \textbf{Equation 10.3}$$

To see how well this model fits, consider Figure 10.3, which contains observed and expected frequencies, residuals, and the predicted probability of a response for each of the log concentrations.

Figure 10.3   Statistics for each concentration

```
Observed and Expected Frequencies

           Number of    Observed    Expected
    DOSE    Subjects    Responses    Responses    Residual     Prob

    1.01      50.0        44.0        45.586       -1.586      .91172
     .89      49.0        42.0        39.330        2.670      .80265
     .71      46.0        24.0        24.845        -.845      .54010
     .58      48.0        16.0        15.816         .184      .32950
     .41      50.0         6.0         6.253        -.253      .12506
```

You can see that the model appears to fit the data reasonably well. A goodness-of-fit test for the model, based on the residuals, is shown in Figure 10.2. The chi-square goodness-of-fit test is calculated as

$$\chi^2 = \sum \frac{(\text{residual}_i)^2}{n_i \hat{P}_i (1 - \hat{P}_i)}$$

Equation 10.4

where n_i is the number of subjects exposed to dose i, and $\hat{P}_i$ is the predicted proportion responding at dose i. The degrees of freedom are equal to the number of doses minus the number of estimated parameters. In this example, we have five doses and two estimated parameters, so there are three degrees of freedom for the chi-square statistic. Since the observed significance level for the chi-square statistic is large—0.655—there is no reason to doubt the model.

When the significance level of the chi-square statistic is small, several explanations are possible. It may be that the relationship between the concentration and the probit is not linear. Or it may be that the relationship is linear but the spread of the observed points around the regression line is unequal. That is, the data are heterogeneous. If this is the case, a correction must be applied to the estimated variances for each concentration group (see "Confidence Intervals for Expected Dosages" below).

Confidence Intervals for Expected Dosages

Often you want to know what the concentration of an agent must be in order to achieve a certain proportion of response. For example, you may want to know what the concentration would have to be in order to kill half of the insects. This is known as the **median lethal dose**. It can be obtained from the previous regression equation by solving for the concentration that corresponds to a probit value of 0. For this example,

$$\log_{10}(\text{median lethal dose}) = 2.86/4.17$$

$$\text{median lethal dose} = 4.85$$

Equation 10.5

Confidence intervals can be constructed for the median lethal dose as well as for the dose required to achieve any response. The SPSS Probit Analysis procedure calculates 95% intervals for the concentrations required to achieve various levels of response. The values for this example are shown in Figure 10.4.

Figure 10.4 Confidence intervals

`Confidence Limits for Effective DOSE`

Prob	DOSE	95% Confidence Limits	
		Lower	Upper
.01	1.34232	.90152	1.73955
.02	1.56042	1.09195	1.97144
.03	1.71682	1.23282	2.13489
.04	1.84473	1.35041	2.26709
.05	1.95577	1.45411	2.38094
.06	2.05553	1.54847	2.48260
.07	2.14718	1.63607	2.57552
.08	2.23270	1.71858	2.66189
.09	2.31344	1.79709	2.74314
.10	2.39033	1.87239	2.82033
.15	2.73686	2.21737	3.16638
.20	3.04775	2.53300	3.47603
.25	3.34246	2.83556	3.77074
.30	3.63134	3.13342	4.06251
.35	3.92126	3.43173	4.36004
.40	4.21775	3.73415	4.67105
.45	4.52592	4.04368	5.00346
.50	4.85119	4.36322	5.36609
.55	5.19983	4.69624	5.76942
.60	5.57976	5.04753	6.22651
.65	6.00164	5.42413	6.75456
.70	6.48081	5.83681	7.37806
.75	7.04092	6.30250	8.13488
.80	7.72177	6.84956	9.08968
.85	8.59893	7.53102	10.36751
.90	9.84550	8.46614	12.26163
.91	10.17274	8.70644	12.77237
.92	10.54059	8.97434	13.35269
.93	10.96042	9.27744	14.02276
.94	11.44911	9.62693	14.81270
.95	12.03312	10.04028	15.77021
.96	12.75742	10.54699	16.97720
.97	13.70788	11.20286	18.59208
.98	15.08186	12.13489	20.98491
.99	17.53233	13.75688	25.40958

The column labeled *Prob* is the proportion responding. The column labeled *DOSE* is the estimated dosage required to achieve this proportion. The 95% confidence limits for the dose are shown in the next two columns. If the chi-square goodness-of-fit test has a significance level less than 0.15 (the program default), a heterogeneity correction is automatically included in the computation of the intervals (Finney, 1971).

Comparing Several Groups

In the previous example, only one stimulus at several doses was studied. If you want to compare several different stimuli, each measured at several doses, additional statistics may be useful. Consider the inclusion of two additional insecticides in the previously described problem. Besides rotenone at five concentrations, we also have five concentrations of deguelin and four concentrations of a mixture of the two. Figure 10.5 shows a partial listing of these data, as entered in the Data Editor. As in the previous example, variable *dose* contains the insecticide concentration, *total* contains the total number of cases, and *died* contains the number of deaths. Factor variable *agent* is coded 1 (roten-one), 2 (deguelin), or 3 (mixture).

Figure 10.5   Data for rotenone and deguelin

	dose	agent	total	died
1	2.57	1.00	50.00	6.00
2	3.80	1.00	48.00	16.00
3	5.13	1.00	46.00	24.00
4	7.76	1.00	49.00	42.00
5	10.23	1.00	50.00	44.00
6	10.00	2.00	48.00	18.00
7	20.42	2.00	48.00	34.00
8	30.20	2.00	49.00	47.00
9	40.74	2.00	50.00	47.00
10	50.12	2.00	48.00	48.00

Figure 10.6 is a plot of the observed probits against the logs of the concentrations for each of the three groups separately.

Figure 10.6   Plot of observed probits against logs of concentrations

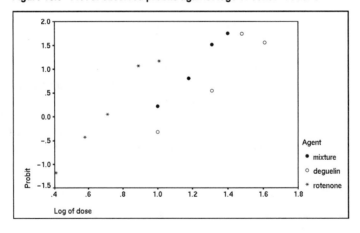

You can see that there appears to be a linear relationship between the two variables for all three groups. One of the questions of interest is whether all three lines are parallel. If so, it would make sense to estimate a common slope for them. Figure 10.7 contains the estimate of the common slope, separate intercept estimates for each of the groups, and a test of parallelism.

Figure 10.7 Intercept estimates and test of parallelism

	Regression Coeff.	Standard Error	Coeff./S.E.	
DOSE	3.90635	.30691	12.72803	

	Intercept	Standard Error	Intercept/S.E.	AGENT
	-2.67343	.23577	-11.33913	rotenone
	-4.36573	.40722	-10.72071	deguelin
	-3.71153	.37491	-9.89977	mixture

```
Pearson  Goodness-of-Fit  Chi Square =     7.471   DF = 24   P =  .999
         PARALLELISM TEST CHI SQUARE =     1.162   DF = 2    P =  .559
```

Since Goodness-of-Fit Chi square is NOT significant, no heterogeneity factor is used in the calculation of confidence limits.

The observed significance level for the test of parallelism is large—0.559—so there is no reason to reject the hypothesis that all three lines are parallel. Thus, the equation for rotenone is estimated to be

$$\text{Probit}(P_i) = -2.67 + 3.91(\log_{10}(\text{dose}_i)) \qquad \textbf{Equation 10.6}$$

The equation for deguelin is

$$\text{Probit}(P_i) = -4.37 + 3.91(\log_{10}(\text{dose}_i)) \qquad \textbf{Equation 10.7}$$

and the equation for the mixture is

$$\text{Probit}(P_i) = -3.71 + 3.91(\log_{10}(\text{dose}_i)) \qquad \textbf{Equation 10.8}$$

Comparing Relative Potencies of the Agents

The relative potency of two stimuli is defined as the ratio of two doses that are equally effective. For example, the relative median potency is the ratio of two doses that achieve a response rate of 50%. In the case of parallel regression lines, there is a constant relative potency at all levels of response. For example, consider Figure 10.8, which shows some of the doses needed to achieve a particular response for each of the three agents.

Figure 10.8 Expected doses

```
AGENT      1  rotenone

                          95% Confidence Limits
Prob          DOSE       Lower          Upper

.25        3.24875     2.82553        3.65426
.30        3.54926     3.11581        3.97227
.35        3.85249     3.40758        4.29636
.40        4.16414     3.70545        4.63356
.45        4.48965     4.01370        4.99083
.50        4.83482     4.33680        5.37586
.55        5.20654     4.68002        5.79788
.60        5.61352     5.05003        6.26880
.65        6.06764     5.45592        6.80487
.70        6.58603     5.91086        7.42974
.75        7.19524     6.43524        8.18030

AGENT      2  deguelin

                          95% Confidence Limits
Prob          DOSE       Lower          Upper

.25        8.80913     7.24085       10.32755
.30        9.62399     8.00041       11.20430
.35       10.44620     8.76976       12.09054
.40       11.29127     9.56202       13.00451
.45       12.17389    10.38960       13.96387
.50       13.10986    11.26577       14.98799
.55       14.11778    12.20605       16.10010
.60       15.22135    13.23000       17.33026
.65       16.45271    14.36393       18.71981
.70       17.85833    15.64554       20.32922
.75       19.51024    17.13277       22.25327

AGENT      3  mixture

                          95% Confidence Limits
Prob          DOSE       Lower          Upper

.25        5.99049     4.82754        7.12052
.30        6.54462     5.33737        7.72006
.35        7.10375     5.85480        8.32478
.40        7.67843     6.38880        8.94696
.45        8.27864     6.94795        9.59841
.50        8.91512     7.54150       10.29194
.55        9.60054     8.18034       11.04290
.60       10.35100     8.87822       11.87107
.65       11.18837     9.65364       12.80367
.70       12.14424    10.53309       13.88054
.75       13.26759    11.55720       15.16421
```

For rotenone, the expected dosage to kill half of the insects is 4.83; for deguelin, it is 13.11; and for the mixture, it is 8.91. The relative median potency for rotenone compared to deguelin is 4.83/13.11 , or 0.37; for rotenone compared to the mixture, it is 0.54; and for deguelin compared to the mixture, it is 1.47. These relative median potencies and their confidence intervals are shown in Figure 10.9.

Figure 10.9   Relative potencies and their confidence intervals

```
Estimates of Relative Median Potency


                               95% Confidence Limits
     AGENT       Estimate      Lower        Upper

     1 VS.  2      .3688       .23353       .52071
     1 VS.  3      .5423       .38085       .71248
     2 VS.  3     1.4705      1.20619      1.85007
```

If a confidence interval does not include the value of 1, we have reason to suspect the hypothesis that the two agents are equally potent.

Estimating the Natural Response Rate

In some situations, the response of interest is expected to occur even if the stimulus is not present. For example, if the organism of interest has a very short life span, you would expect to observe deaths even without the agent. In such situations, you must adjust the observed proportions to reflect deaths due to the agent alone.

If the natural response rate is known, it can be entered into the SPSS Probit Analysis procedure. It can also be estimated from the data, provided that data for a dose of 0 are entered together with the other doses. If the natural response rate is estimated from the data, an additional degree of freedom must be subtracted from the chi-square goodness-of-fit degrees of freedom.

More than One Stimulus Variable

If several stimuli are evaluated simultaneously, an additional term is added to the regression model for each stimulus. Regression coefficients and standard errors are displayed for each stimulus. In the case of several stimuli, relative potencies and confidence intervals for the doses needed to achieve a particular response cannot be calculated in the usual fashion, since you need to consider various combinations of the levels of the stimuli.

11

Nonlinear Regression Examples

Many real-world relationships are approximated with linear models, especially in the absence of theoretical models that can serve as guides. We would be unwise to model the relationship between speed of a vehicle and stopping time with a linear model, since the laws of physics dictate otherwise. However, nothing deters us from modeling salary as a linear function of variables such as age, education, and experience. In general, we choose the simplest model that fits an observed relationship. Another reason that explains our affinity to linear models is the accompanying simplicity of statistical estimation and hypothesis testing. Algorithms for estimating parameters of linear models are straightforward; direct solutions are available; iteration is not required. There are, however, situations in which it is necessary to fit nonlinear models. Before considering the steps involved in nonlinear model estimation, let's consider what makes a model nonlinear.

What Is a Nonlinear Model?

There is often confusion about the characteristics of a nonlinear model. Consider the following equation:

$$Y = B_0 + B_1 X_1^2$$

Equation 11.1

Is this a linear or nonlinear model? The equation is certainly not that of a straight line—it is the equation for a parabola. However, the word *linear*, in this context, does not refer to whether the equation is that of a straight line or a curve. It refers to the functional form of the equation. That is, can the dependent variable be expressed as a linear combination of parameter values times values of the independent variables? The parameters must be linear. The independent variables can be transformed in any fashion. They can be raised to various powers, logged, and so on. The transformation cannot involve the parameters in any way, however.

The previous model is a linear model, since it is nonlinear in only the independent variable X. It is linear in the parameters B_0 and B_1. In fact, we can write the model as

$$Y = B_0 + B_1 X'$$

Equation 11.2

where X' is the square of X_1. The parameters in the model can be estimated using the usual linear model techniques.

Transforming Nonlinear Models

Consider the model

$$Y = e^{B_0 + B_1 X_1 + B_2 X_2 + E}$$

Equation 11.3

The model, as it stands, is not of the form

$$Y = B_0 + B_1 Z_1 + B_2 Z_2 + \ldots + B_p Z_p + E$$

Equation 11.4

where the B's are the parameters and the Z's are functions of the independent variables, so it is a nonlinear model. However, if we take natural logs of both sides of Equation 11.3, we get the model

$$\ln(Y) = B_0 + B_1 X_1 + B_2 X_2 + E$$

Equation 11.5

The transformed equation is linear in the parameters, and we can use the usual techniques for estimating them. Models that initially appear to be nonlinear but that can be transformed to a linear form are sometimes called **intrinsically linear models**. It is a good idea to examine what appears to be a nonlinear model to see if it can be transformed to a linear one. Transformation to linearity makes estimation much easier.

Another example of a transformable nonlinear model is

$$Y = e^B X + E$$

Equation 11.6

The transformation $B' = e^B$ results in the model

$$Y = B' X + E$$

Equation 11.7

We can use the usual methods to estimate B' and then take its natural log to get the values of B.

Error Terms in Transformed Models

In both linear and nonlinear models, we assume that the error term is additive. When we transform a model to linearity, we must make sure that the transformed error term satisfies the requisite assumptions. For example, if our original model is

$$Y = e^{BX} + E$$

Equation 11.8

taking natural logs does not result in a model that has an additive error term. To have an additive error term in the transformed model, our original model would have had to be

$$Y = e^{BX + E} = e^{BX}e^{E}$$

Equation 11.9

Intrinsically Nonlinear Models

A model such as

$$Y = B_0 + e^{B_1 X_1} + e^{B_2 X_2} + e^{B_3 X_3} + E$$

Equation 11.10

is **intrinsically nonlinear**. We can't apply a transformation to linearize it. We must estimate the parameters using nonlinear regression. In nonlinear regression, just as in linear regression, we choose values for the parameters so that the sum of squared residuals is a minimum. There is not, however, a closed solution. We must solve for the values iteratively. There are several algorithms for the estimation of nonlinear models (see Fox, 1984; Draper and Smith, 1981).

Fitting the Logistic Population Growth Model

As an example of fitting a nonlinear equation, we will consider a model for population growth. Population growth is often modeled using a logistic population growth model of the form

$$Y_i = \frac{C}{1 + e^{A + BT_i}} + E_i$$

Equation 11.11

where Y_i is the population size at time T_i. Although the model often fits the observed data reasonably well, the assumptions of independent error and constant variance may be violated because, with time series data, errors are not independent and the size of the error may be dependent on the magnitude of the population. Since the logistic population growth model is not transformable to a linear model, we will have to use nonlinear regression to estimate the parameters.

Figure 11.1 contains a listing of decennial populations (in millions) of the United States from 1790 to 1960, as found in Fox (1984). Figure 11.2 is a plot of the same data. For the nonlinear regression, we will use the variable *decade*, which represents the number of decades since 1790, as the independent variable. This should prevent possible computational difficulties arising from large data values (see "Computational Problems" on p. 102).

Figure 11.1   Decennial population of the United States

```
POP YEAR DECADE

  3.895 1790      0
  5.267 1800      1
  7.182 1810      2
  9.566 1820      3
 12.834 1830      4
 16.985 1840      5
 23.069 1850      6
 31.278 1860      7
 38.416 1870      8
 49.924 1880      9
 62.692 1890     10
 75.734 1900     11
 91.812 1910     12
109.806 1920     13
122.775 1930     14
131.669 1940     15
150.697 1950     16
178.464 1960     17
```

Figure 11.2   Plot of decennial population of the United States

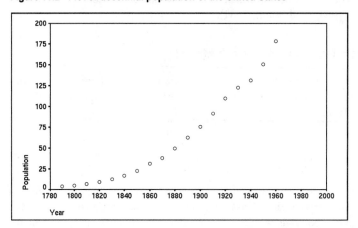

In order to start the nonlinear estimation algorithm, we must have initial values for the parameters. Unfortunately, the results of nonlinear estimation often depend on having good starting values for the parameters. There are several ways for obtaining starting values (see "Estimating Starting Values" on p. 100 through "Use Properties of the Nonlinear Model" on p. 101).

For this example, we can obtain starting values by making some simple assumptions. In the logistic growth model, the parameter *C* represents the asymptote. We'll arbitrarily choose an asymptote that is not too far from the largest observed value. Let's take an asymptote of 200, since the largest observed value for the population is 178.

Using the value of 200 for *C*, we can estimate a value for *A* based on the observed population at time 0:

$$3.895 = \frac{200}{1 + e^A}$$

Equation 11.12

So,

$$A = \ln\left(\frac{200}{3.895} - 1\right) = 3.9$$

Equation 11.13

To estimate a value for *B*, we can use the population at time 1, and our estimates of *C* and *A*. This gives us

$$5.267 = \frac{200}{1 + e^{B + 3.9}}$$

Equation 11.14

from which we derive

$$B = \ln\left(\frac{200}{5.27} - 1\right) - 3.9 = -0.29$$

Equation 11.15

We use these values as initial values in the nonlinear regression routine.

Estimating the Parameters

Figure 11.3 shows the residual sums of squares and parameter estimates at each iteration. At step 1, the parameter estimates are the starting values that we have supplied. At the major iterations, which are identified with integer numbers, the derivatives are evaluated and the direction of the search determined. At the minor iterations, the distance is established. As the note at the end of the table indicates, iteration stops when the relative change in residual sums of squares between iterations is less than or equal to the convergence criterion.

Figure 11.3   Parameter estimates for nonlinear regression

```
Iteration  Residual SS          A           B           C

    1       969.6898219   3.90000000   -.30000000   200.000000
    1.1     240.3756627   3.87148504   -.27852485   237.513990
    2       240.3756627   3.87148504   -.27852485   237.513990
    2.1     186.5020615   3.89003377   -.27910189   243.721558
    3       186.5020615   3.89003377   -.27910189   243.721558
    3.1     186.4972404   3.88880287   -.27886478   243.975460
    4       186.4972404   3.88880287   -.27886478   243.975460
    4.1     186.4972278   3.88885123   -.27886164   243.985980
    5       186.4972278   3.88885123   -.27886164   243.985980
    5.1     186.4972277   3.88884856   -.27886059   243.987296
```

Run stopped after 10 model evaluations and 5 derivative evaluations.
Iterations have been stopped because the relative reduction between successive
residual sums of squares is at most SSCON = 1.000E-08

Summary statistics for the nonlinear regression are shown in Figure 11.4. For a nonlinear model, the tests used for linear models are not appropriate. In this situation, the residual mean square is not an unbiased estimate of the error variance, even if the model is correct. For practical purposes, we can still compare the residual variance with an estimate of the total variance, but the usual *F* statistic cannot be used for testing hypotheses.

The entry in Figure 11.4 labeled *Uncorrected Total* is the sum of the squared values of the dependent variable. The entry labeled *(Corrected Total)* is the sum of squared deviations around the mean. The *Regression* sum of squares is the sum of the squared predicted values. The entry labeled *R squared* is the coefficient of determination. It may be interpreted as the proportion of the total variation of the dependent variable around its mean that is explained by the fitted model. For nonlinear models, its value can be negative if the selected model fits worse than the mean. (For a discussion of this statistic, see Kvalseth, 1985.) It appears from the R^2 value of 0.9965 that the model fits the observed values well. Figure 11.5 is a plot of the observed and predicted values for the model.

Figure 11.4   Summary statistics for nonlinear regression

```
Nonlinear Regression Summary Statistics      Dependent Variable POP

   Source               DF  Sum of Squares  Mean Square

   Regression            3   123053.53112    41017.84371
   Residual             15      186.49723       12.43315
   Uncorrected Total    18   123240.02834

   (Corrected Total)    17    53293.92477

   R squared = 1 - Residual SS / Corrected SS =     .99650
```

Figure 11.5   Observed and predicted values for nonlinear model

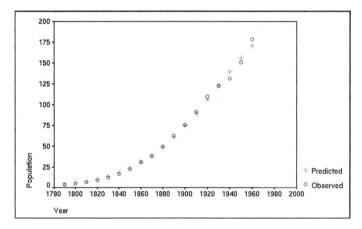

Approximate Confidence Intervals for the Parameters

In the case of nonlinear regression, it is not possible to obtain exact confidence intervals for each of the parameters. Instead, we must rely on **asymptotic** (large sample) approximations. Figure 11.6 shows the estimated parameters, standard errors, and asymptotic 95% confidence intervals. The asymptotic correlation matrix of the parameter estimates is shown in Figure 11.7. If there are very large positive or negative values for the correlation coefficients, it is possible that the model is **overparameterized**. That is, a model with fewer parameters may fit the observed data as well. This does not necessarily mean that the model is inappropriate; it may mean that the amount of data is not sufficient to estimate all of the parameters.

Figure 11.6   Estimated parameters and confidence intervals

Parameter	Estimate	Asymptotic Std. Error	Asymptotic 95 % Confidence Interval Lower	Upper
A	3.888848562	.093704407	3.689122346	4.088574778
B	-.278860588	.015593951	-.312098308	-.245622868
C	243.98729636	17.967399750	205.69069033	282.28390239

Figure 11.7   Asymptotic correlation matrix of parameter estimates

Asymptotic Correlation Matrix of the Parameter Estimates

	A	B	C
A	1.0000	-.7244	-.3762
B	-.7244	1.0000	.9042
C	-.3762	.9042	1.0000

Examining the Residuals

The SPSS Nonlinear Regression procedure allows you to save predicted values and residuals that can be used for exploring the goodness of fit of the model. Figure 11.8 is a plot of residuals against the observed year values. You will note that the errors appear to be correlated and that the variance of the residuals increases with time.

Figure 11.8   Plot of residuals against observed values

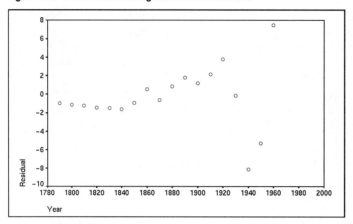

To compute asymptotic standard errors of the predicted values and statistics used for outlier detection and influential case analysis, you can use the SPSS Linear Regression procedure, specifying the residuals from the SPSS Nonlinear Regression procedure as the dependent variable and the derivatives as the independent variables.

Estimating Starting Values

As previously indicated, you must specify initial values for all parameters. Good initial values are important and may provide a better solution in fewer iterations. In addition, computational difficulties can sometimes be avoided by a good choice of initial values. Poor initial values can result in nonconvergence, a local rather than global solution, or a physically impossible solution.

There are a number of ways to determine initial values for nonlinear models. Milliken (1987) and Draper and Smith (1981) describe several approaches, which are summarized in the following sections. Generally, a combination of techniques will be most useful. If you don't have starting values, don't just set them all to 0. Use values in the neighborhood of what you expect to see.

If you ignore the error term, sometimes a linear form of the model can be derived. Linear regression can then be used to obtain initial values. For example, consider the model

$$Y = e^{A + BX} + E \qquad\qquad \textbf{Equation 11.16}$$

If we ignore the error term and take the natural log of both sides of the equation, we obtain the model

$$\ln(Y) = A + BX$$ **Equation 11.17**

We can use linear regression to estimate A and B and specify these values as starting values in nonlinear regression.

Use Properties of the Nonlinear Model

Sometimes we know the values of the dependent variable for certain combinations of parameter values. For example, if in the model

$$Y = e^{A + BX}$$ **Equation 11.18**

we know that when X is 0, Y is 2, we would select the natural log of 2 as a starting value for A. Examination of an equation at its maximum, minimum, and when all the independent variables approach 0 or infinity may help in selection of initial values.

Solve a System of Equations

By taking as many data points as you have parameters, you can solve a simultaneous system of equations. For example, in the previous model, we could solve the equations

$$\ln(Y_1) = A + BX_1$$
$$\ln(Y_2) = A + BX_2$$ **Equation 11.19**

Using subtraction,

$$\ln(Y_1) - \ln(Y_2) = BX_1 - BX_2$$ **Equation 11.20**

we can solve for the values of the parameters

$$B = \frac{\ln(Y_1) - \ln(Y_2)}{X_1 - X_2}$$ **Equation 11.21**

and

$$A = \ln(Y_1) - BX_1$$ **Equation 11.22**

Computational Problems

Computationally, nonlinear regression problems can be difficult to solve. Models that require exponentiation or powers of large data values may cause underflows or over-flows. (An **overflow** is caused by a number that is too large for the computer to handle, while an **underflow** is caused by a number that is too small for the computer to handle.) Sometimes the program may continue and produce a reasonable solution, especially if only a few data points caused the problem. If this is not the case, you must eliminate the cause of the problem. If your data values are large—for example, years—you can sub-tract the smallest year from all of the values. That's what was done with the population example. Instead of using the actual years, we used decades since 1790 (to compute the number of decades, we subtracted the smallest year from each year value and divided the result by 10). You must, however, consider the effect of rescaling on the parameter values. Many nonlinear models are not scale invariant. You can also consider rescaling the parameter values.

If the program fails to arrive at a solution—that is, if it doesn't converge—you might consider choosing different starting values. You can also change the criterion used for convergence.

If none of these strategies works, you can use the sequential quadratic programming algorithm to try to solve problems that are causing difficulties in the Nonlinear Regres-sion procedure, which uses a Levenberg-Marquardt algorithm by default. For a particu-lar problem, one algorithm may perform better than the other.

Additional Nonlinear Regression Options

Three additional options are available for nonlinear models when the sequential quadrat-ic programming algorithm is used. You can supply linear and nonlinear constraints for the values of the parameter estimates, and you can specify your own loss function. (By default, the loss function that is minimized is the sum of the squared residuals.) In addi-tion, standard errors for the parameter estimates as well as asymptotic confidence inter-vals can be obtained with **bootstrapping**, in which repeated random samples are selected from the data and the model is estimated from each one.

12 Weighted Least-Squares Regression Examples

When you estimate the parameters of a linear regression model, all observations usually contribute equally to the computations. This is called **ordinary least-squares (OLS) regression**. When all of the observations have the same variance, this is the best strategy because it results in parameter estimates that have the smallest possible variances. However, if the observations are not measured with equal precision, OLS no longer yields parameter estimates with the smallest variance. A modification known as **weighted least-squares (WLS) analysis** does. In weighted least-squares regression, data points are weighted by the reciprocal of their variances. This means that observations with large variances have less impact on the analysis than observations associated with small variances.

An Example

As an example of the use of weighted least squares, consider the data presented in Table 2.1 of Draper and Smith (1981). Figure 12.1 is a plot of the two variables.

Figure 12.1 Plot of y and x

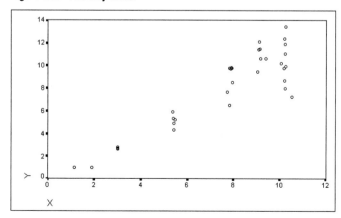

One of the first things you notice is that the variability or spread of the dependent variable increases with increasing values of the independent variable. This indicates that the assumption of equal variances across all data points is probably violated and the ordinary least-squares approach is no longer optimal.

If you were to fit an ordinary least-squares regression to the data points (by running the Linear Regression procedure), you would obtain the output shown in Figure 12.2.

Figure 12.2 Linear Regression output

```
Multiple R               .91659
R Square                 .84013
Adjusted R Square        .83529
Standard Error          1.45660


Analysis of Variance
                     DF      Sum of Squares      Mean Square
Regression            1            367.94805        367.94805
Residual             33             70.01571          2.12169

F =       173.42230      Signif F =   .0000

----------------- Variables in the Equation -----------------

Variable              B        SE B       Beta         T   Sig T

X              1.135404     .086218     .916588    13.169   .0000
(Constant)     -.578954     .679186                 -.852   .4001




Residuals Statistics:

                Min      Max      Mean    Std Dev    N

*PRED         .7268   11.3428    7.7569    3.2897    35
*RESID      -4.0928    2.4238     .0000    1.4350    35
*ZPRED      -2.1370    1.0901     .0000    1.0000    35
*ZRESID     -2.8098    1.6640     .0000     .9852    35

Total Cases =        35


From Equation    1:    2 new variables have been created.

    Name        Contents
    ----        --------

    PRE_1       Predicted Value
    RES_1       Residual
```

You can't tell from the coefficients or summary statistics that the requisite regression assumptions are violated. You must examine the residual plots. These are shown in Figure 12.3.

Figure 12.3   Plot of residuals and predicted values

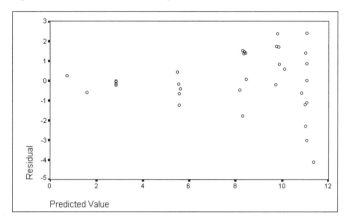

You see that instead of being randomly distributed around the line through 0, the residuals form a funnel, suggesting again that the variances are unequal and that the data
must be transformed (see *SPSS Base User's Guide*) or that weighted least squares
should be used.

Estimating the Weights from Replicates

In order to estimate the regression model with weighted least squares, you must have an
estimate of the variability at each point. Unfortunately, this information is often unavailable and you must estimate the variability from the data. If you have replicates in your
data—that is, groups of cases for which the values of the independent variable are the
same or similar—you can compute the variances of the dependent variable for all of the
distinct combinations of the independent variables. The reciprocal of the variances is
then the weight, since you want points associated with large variances to have less impact than points with smaller variances. If you have few observations at each point, the
variance estimates based on replicates may not be very reliable.

Estimating Weights from a Variable

If you don't estimate weights from replicates, you can look for a relationship between
the variance and the values of other related variables. It is not unusual for the variance
of a dependent variable to be related to the magnitude of an independent variable. For
example, if you are looking at the relationship between income and education, you may
well expect that there will be more variability in income for people with graduate education than for those who did not complete grammar school.

If you think that there is a relationship between the variance of the dependent variable and the value of an independent variable or any other variable you have available, you can use the Weight Estimation procedure to estimate the weights. However, the variance must be proportional to a power of the variable. That is, the relationship must be of the form

variance $\propto$ variable^{power}  **Equation 12.1**

You can specify a power range and an increment, and the program will evaluate the log-likelihood function for all powers within the grid and then select the power corresponding to the largest log-likelihood.

In the Draper and Smith example, if you group cases with similar values for the independent variable and compute their standard deviations, you obtain the plot shown in Figure 12.4.

Figure 12.4   Plot of standard deviation and x

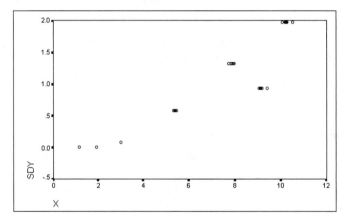

It appears that the standard deviation of y is linearly related to x. That means the variance is related to the square of x.

If you run the Weight Estimation procedure with x as the weight variable and power ranging from 0 to 3 in increments of 0.2, you will obtain the results shown in Figure 12.5.

Figure 12.5 Log-likelihood functions for powers from WLS

```
MODEL:  MOD_1.

Source variable.. X                    Dependent variable.. Y

Log-likelihood Function =  -61.826560    POWER value =    .000
Log-likelihood Function =  -60.591503    POWER value =    .200
Log-likelihood Function =  -59.385889    POWER value =    .400
Log-likelihood Function =  -58.220191    POWER value =    .600
Log-likelihood Function =  -57.108016    POWER value =    .800
Log-likelihood Function =  -56.066817    POWER value =   1.000
Log-likelihood Function =  -55.118623    POWER value =   1.200
Log-likelihood Function =  -54.290631    POWER value =   1.400
Log-likelihood Function =  -53.615443    POWER value =   1.600
Log-likelihood Function =  -53.130626    POWER value =   1.800
Log-likelihood Function =  -52.877225    POWER value =   2.000
Log-likelihood Function =  -52.896965    POWER value =   2.200
Log-likelihood Function =  -53.228140    POWER value =   2.400
Log-likelihood Function =  -53.900705    POWER value =   2.600
Log-likelihood Function =  -54.931654    POWER value =   2.800
Log-likelihood Function =  -56.322024    POWER value =   3.000

The Value of POWER Maximizing Log-likelihood Function =  2.000
```

The largest value of the log-likelihood is for a power of 2, confirming our observation that the variance is related to the square of x.

The WLS Solutions

Figure 12.6 shows the WLS solution when the value of 2 is used for power.

Figure 12.6 Statistics for the best power value

```
Source variable..    X                  POWER value =  2.000

Dependent variable.. Y

Listwise Deletion of Missing Data

Multiple R         .97387
R Square           .94842
Adjusted R Square  .94685
Standard Error     .17292

            Analysis of Variance:

            DF   SUM OF SQUARES      MEAN SQUARE

REGRESSION   1        18.143075        18.143075
RESIDUALS   33          .986776          .029902

F =     606.74502     Signif F =  .0000

----------------- Variables in the Equation -----------------

Variable          B        SE B       Beta        T  Sig T

X          1.130362     .045890    .973867   24.632  .0000
(Constant)  -.580006     .189983             -3.053  .0045

Log-likelihood Function =  -52.877225


The following new variables are being created:

   Name       Label

   WGT#1      Weight for Y from WLS, MOD_1  X** -2.000
```

(The weights that are saved from the procedure are the reciprocals of x^2). You will note that, compared to the OLS results in Figure 12.2, the parameter estimates for the slope and intercept have not changed much. What has changed are their standard deviations. In the OLS solution, the standard deviation of the slope (*SE B*) is 0.086. In the WLS solution, the standard deviation of the slope is 0.046. Similarly, for the constant, the standard deviation has changed from 0.68 to 0.19.

Diagnostics from the Linear Regression Procedure

The Weight Estimation procedure will only estimate weights and provide summary regression statistics. You must use the Linear Regression procedure specifying the weight variable to obtain residuals and other diagnostic information. In fact, if you know the weights, there is no need to run the Weight Estimation procedure; you can perform weighted least-squares analyses using the Linear Regression procedure.

Draper and Smith estimated the weights for the example data by computing variances for cases with similar values of the independent variables. They then developed a quadratic regression model to predict the variances from the values of the independent variable. If you apply their weights using the Linear Regression procedure, you will obtain the summary statistics shown in Figure 12.7.

Figure 12.7   Summary statistics from the Draper and Smith estimated weights

```
Multiple R              .95975
R Square                .92111
Adjusted R Square       .91872
Standard Error         1.13577

Analysis of Variance
                    DF      Sum of Squares      Mean Square
Regression           1           497.04422        497.04422
Residual            33            42.56923          1.28998

F =     385.31256       Signif F =   .0000


----------------- Variables in the Equation -----------------

Variable            B        SE B       Beta        T   Sig T

X            1.164999     .059350    .959746   19.629   .0000
(Constant)   -.888995     .300037              -2.963   .0056


End Block Number   1   All requested variables entered.

NOTE: No plots will be produced when /REGWGT is specified.  You can SAVE the
appropriate variables and use other procedures (e.g.  EXAMINE and PLOT) to
produce the requested plots.  To plot weighted versions of the residuals and
predicted values, use COMPUTE before plotting:
COMPUTE RESID = SQRT(REGWGTvar) * RESID
COMPUTE PRED = SQRT(REGWGTvar) * PRED


From Equation   1:   2 new variables have been created.

    Name       Contents
    ----       --------

    PRE_2      Predicted Value
    RES_2      Residual
```

Note that the slope has changed somewhat from the OLS solution, as has the constant.

This solution also differs from that shown in Figure 12.6. One of the reasons for this difference is that Draper and Smith's weights are not as extreme as those estimated by the WLS procedure using a quadratic source model. Our estimated weights range from 0.75 to 0.0076, while Draper and Smith's range from 0.30 to 7.8. (The actual numbers used for the weights don't matter. All that matters is the proportionality.) The Draper and Smith weights are probably more realistic, since our estimated hundred-fold increase in variance over the observed range of the independent variable is probably too extreme.

To see how well the Draper and Smith WLS solution performs, let's examine the residuals. You must save the residuals and predicted values from the Linear Regression procedure, but you must transform them before plotting. They must be multiplied by the square root of the weight variable.

Figure 12.8 is a plot of the transformed residuals and predicted values.

Figure 12.8   Plot of transformed residuals and predicted values

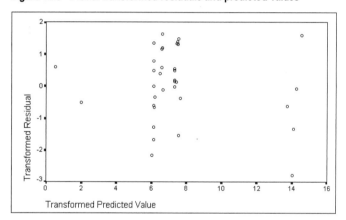

You see that the funnel shape that was evident in Figure 12.3 is no longer as marked. It appears that the WLS solution was successful.

13 Two-Stage Least-Squares Regression Examples

Macroeconomic data—data describing the overall state of the economy—frequently take the form of time series. Because of the complex interrelationships among macroeconomic variables, models for such data are usually afflicted with correlated errors: the errors in the equation are correlated with one or more of the predictor variables. When this is true, estimates made with ordinary least-squares (OLS) regression are biased. In this chapter, we will see how to use the technique known as two-stage least squares to deal with correlated errors using a classic macroeconomic model in a very modest setting.

The Artichoke Data

To illustrate the concepts involved in two-stage least squares, we will use a hypothetical set of data on the production of artichokes from Kelejian and Oates (1989). Three main series are involved in the model: the *demand* for artichokes, expressed as the quantity sold, in tons; the *price* of an artichoke in cents; and the average family *income* in thousands of dollars.

Figure 13.1 Demand, price, and income

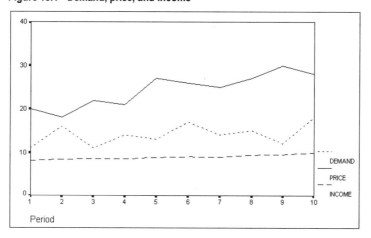

The Demand-Price-Income Economic Model

A classic economic model of the demand for some commodity, such as artichokes, is expressed as the following:

$$\text{DEMAND} = \beta_0 + \beta_1 \times \text{PRICE} + \beta_2 \times \text{INCOME} + \text{Error}$$ **Equation 13.1**

The path diagram shown in Figure 13.2 represents this equation.

Figure 13.2   Path diagram for simple model

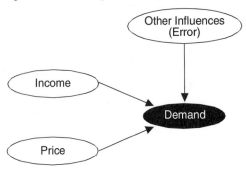

Although there is more to the model than this one equation, let's go ahead and estimate the coefficients using ordinary least-squares regression.

Estimation with Ordinary Least Squares

Figure 13.3 shows an ordinary least-squares (OLS) estimation of the model in Equation 13.1. This model estimates that an extra thousand dollars of mean family income increases the demand for artichokes by about 6.2 tons, while each extra penny in the price of artichokes decreases the demand by about 0.66 tons. Since Kelejian and Oates's data are hypothetical, we will not dwell on the interpretation of the coefficients. Instead, let us consider some difficulties with models such as the one in Equation 13.1.

Figure 13.3   OLS estimation of artichoke production

```
* * * *   M U L T I P L E    R E G R E S S I O N   * * * *

Listwise Deletion of Missing Data

Equation Number 1    Dependent Variable..   DEMAND

Block Number  1.  Method: Enter    PRICE    INCOME


Variable(s) Entered on Step Number  1..    INCOME
                                    2..    PRICE


Multiple R            .73832      Analysis of Variance
R Square              .54512                     DF    Sum of Squares    Mean Square
Adjusted R Square     .41516      Regression      2          28.83688       14.41844
Standard Error       1.85407      Residual        7          24.06312        3.43759

                                  F =      4.19435    Signif F =  .0635


----------------- Variables in the Equation -----------------

Variable             B          SE B        Beta         T   Sig T

PRICE           -.658904     .316896   -1.065767    -2.079   .0762
INCOME         6.208855    2.212209    1.438609     2.807   .0263
(Constant)   -25.081550   13.550746                -1.851   .1066


End Block Number   1   All requested variables entered.
```


Feedback and Correlated Errors

The difficulty with a model relating production, price, and income is that the influences
work in both directions. Equation 13.1 states that the quantity of artichokes produced depends upon the price—when prices are high, farmers tend to grow more artichokes. It is
equally true that the price depends upon production—a glut of artichokes on the market
will force prices back down. (The model assumes that, at the market price, the demand
for artichokes equals supply.) Thus, we should regard Equation 13.1 as part of a system
of interrelated equations. The OLS solution shown above ignored the feedback effect of
production on price. The real situation is more like the one shown in Figure 13.4.

Figure 13.4 Path diagram showing feedback

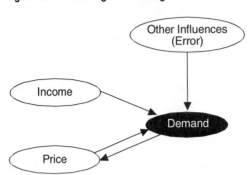

Suppose that something not included in the model (a new fertilizer, perhaps) leads to an increased quantity of artichokes on the market. Prices will fall due to the increased production. Because of the feedback relationship, high values of the error term in Figure 13.4 (which represents the effect of things not included in the equation) would be associated with low prices of artichokes.

Correlation of the error term with one of the predictor variables violates one of the assumptions of regression analysis. It leads to biased coefficients because the model in Figure 13.2 implies that price levels cause increased production. The OLS algorithm used by the Linear Regression procedure treats that portion of the error that is correlated with *price* as being caused by *price*—although really the correlation arises in the other direction, from the feedback effect of *demand* on *price*.

Note that it is the *theoretical* errors that are correlated with the predictor *price*. If you actually use the Linear Regression procedure, the OLS algorithm assumes the errors to be uncorrelated with the predictors and calculates biased coefficients in such a way as to produce uncorrelated residuals. Thus, you cannot use the estimated errors produced by a regression procedure to *check* for the problem of correlated errors. You know the correlated errors are there because of the feedback loop in the correctly specified model.

Two-Stage Least Squares

We know there are problems with the ordinary least-squares analysis presented above. The feedback relationship from the dependent variable *demand* to the predictor variable *price* produces correlations between the error term in Equation 13.1 and *price*, and therefore the estimates from OLS regression are biased.

Two-stage least squares (2SLS) is an important regression technique for models in which one (or more) of the predictor variables is thought to be correlated with the error term. Before we discuss 2SLS strategy, we need to introduce some terminology.

Endogenous Variables. Endogenous literally means *produced from within.* In regression analysis, an endogenous variable is a variable that is causally dependent on the other variable(s) in the model. When you are specifying models that solve several equations simultaneously (whether or not you explicitly solve all the equations), you know that several endogenous variables are present.

In a feedback situation, each of the variables in the feedback relationship is endogenous. Thus, in the model of Equation 13.1, *price* and *demand* are endogenous variables. The model should include the two-way relationship between *price* and *demand*, as in Figure 13.4.

Instruments. Instrumental variables, or simply *instruments,* are variables that are not influenced by other variables in the model but that do influence those variables. They may or may not be a part of the equation you are interested in, but they must be free of causal influence from any of the variables in that equation. To be effective, instruments should be:

- Highly correlated with the endogenous variables.

- Not correlated with the error terms.

A third, practical consideration is that the instrumental variables must be available for use in your analysis.

In Figure 13.5, you can see that there is a path *from* the instruments to the endogenous variable *price*, but that no paths lead *to* the instruments from the rest of the model.

Figure 13.5 Instrument variables

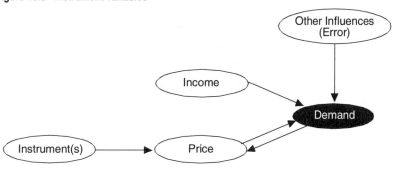

In practice, it is difficult to be sure whether an instrument is correlated with the (unobserved) error term. As noted in "Feedback and Correlated Errors" on p. 113, you cannot test this by using the estimated error terms from the Linear Regression procedure. When no instrument is readily available, the lagged value of the endogenous variable is often used. Even if this is correlated with the lagged error, it may not be correlated with the current error.

Strategy

In two-stage least squares, you are faced with a situation where an endogenous predictor variable (*price*) is correlated with the theoretical error terms in your model for the dependent variable (*demand*). OLS wrongly attributes some of the theoretically unexplained variation in *demand* to the effect of *price* because of this correlation. The 2SLS strategy is to replace the troublesome endogenous predictor variable *price* with a similar variable that:

- Is almost as good as *price* at predicting *demand*.
- Is not correlated with the theoretical error term in the prediction of *demand*.

You obtain such a replacement variable by ordinary regression, using the instruments to predict the endogenous variable. If the instruments have the two properties listed in "Two-Stage Least Squares" on p. 114, the predicted value of the endogenous variable will be:

- A good predictor of the dependent variable.
- Uncorrelated with the error term for the dependent variable.

To appreciate what is involved in two-stage least squares, we will work through the very simple demand-for-artichokes example using the Linear Regression procedure (in two stages). We will then see how the 2-Stage Least Squares procedure automates the process.

Stage 1: Estimating Price

The first stage requires instruments with which to predict *price*. If the instruments are not affected by *demand*, then the predicted values of *price* will likewise be unaffected by *demand* and we can safely use those predicted values in the second stage.

The instruments we will use are:

- *income*. This is one of the predictor variables in Equation 13.1. It is unlikely that the demand for artichokes affects the income of consumers in any large way, but it is possible that income levels will be useful in predicting price levels.
- *rainfall*. This variable is not a part of Equation 13.1 because we do not expect it to be useful in predicting the demand for artichokes. It should affect the price of artichokes, however, because of its effect on the quantity available. Since it is unlikely to be influenced by demand (or anything else), it is a suitable instrument.
- Lagged *price*. The lagged value of an endogenous variable is very often used as an instrument because it is frequently a good predictor of the current value. You have good reason to believe that the current demand for artichokes does not affect last season's price, so lagged price should be uncorrelated with the errors in the demand model.

The first stage of the estimation, using these instruments, is shown in Figure 13.6. The predicted values of *price* from this equation are saved in a new series named *pre_1*.

Figure 13.6   Using instruments to predict price

```
* * * *   M U L T I P L E   R E G R E S S I O N   * * * *
```

Listwise Deletion of Missing Data

Equation Number 1   Dependent Variable..   PRICE

Block Number 1. Method: Enter   INCOME   RAINFALL LAGPRICE

Variable(s) Entered on Step Number 1..   LAGPRICE LAGS(PRICE,1) on 29 Apr 93 at 15:34
                                   2..   RAINFALL
                                   3..   INCOME

```
Multiple R            .91854     Analysis of Variance
R Square              .84372                    DF    Sum of Squares    Mean Square
Adjusted R Square     .74996     Regression      3          98.62173       32.87391
Standard Error       1.91140     Residual        5          18.26716        3.65343

                                 F =      8.99809    Signif F =  .0185
```

----------------- Variables in the Equation ------------------

```
Variable          B          SE B       Beta        T   Sig T

INCOME        3.752000    2.994052    .506352    1.253  .2656
RAINFALL      -.217927     .105674   -.442332   -2.062  .0942
LAGPRICE       .418053     .417602    .430582    1.001  .3627
(Constant)   -8.579676   20.892358              -.411  .6983
```

End Block Number   1   All requested variables entered.

```
* * * *   M U L T I P L E   R E G R E S S I O N   * * * *
```

Equation Number 1   Dependent Variable..   PRICE

Residuals Statistics:

```
            Min       Max     Mean   Std Dev   N

*PRED    18.6584   29.8526  24.8889   3.5111   9
*RESID   -1.7745    2.7180    .0000   1.5111   9
*ZPRED   -1.7745    1.4137    .0000   1.0000   9
*ZRESID   -.9284    1.4220    .0000    .7906   9
```

Total Cases =   10

```
* * * * * * * * * * * * * * * * * * * * * * * * * * * * * *
```

From Equation   1:   1 new variables have been created.

```
  Name        Contents
  ----        --------

  PRE_1       Predicted Value
```

Stage 2: Estimating the Model

The second stage is to estimate the model we are interested in (Equation 13.1) with *pre_1* substituted for *price*. Figure 13.7 shows this procedure.

The regression coefficients in Figure 13.7 are the ones we want—the ones that belong in Equation 13.1, given what we know about feedback in the overall model. The coefficient of *income* is 9.561, and the coefficient of *price* is –1.265. Notice that both coefficients have changed appreciably from Figure 13.3, where we used ordinary least squares to estimate them.

Figure 13.7   Using pre_1 to predict demand

```
              * * * *    M U L T I P L E    R E G R E S S I O N    * * * *

Listwise Deletion of Missing Data

Equation Number 1    Dependent Variable..    DEMAND

Block Number  1.  Method:  Enter       PRE_1 INCOME

Variable(s) Entered on Step Number  1..    INCOME
                                    2..    PRE_1  Predicted Value

Multiple R            .85655     Analysis of Variance
R Square              .73368                       DF    Sum of Squares    Mean Square
Adjusted R Square     .64490     Regression         2          30.97742       15.48871
Standard Error       1.36899     Residual           6          11.24480        1.87413

                                 F =      8.26446      Signif F =  .0189


----------------- Variables in the Equation -----------------

Variable            B        SE B       Beta        T   Sig T

PRE_1         -1.265008    .345830  -1.933343    -3.658   .0106
INCOME         9.561323   2.353817   2.146960     4.062   .0066
(Constant)   -40.016582  13.708401               -2.919   .0267

End Block Number   1   All requested variables entered.
```

However, the R^2 and the standard errors reported in Figure 13.7 are not the ones we want. This is because Figure 13.7 shows an equation with *pre_1*, but we want the R^2 and standard errors for Equation 13.1, which uses *price*. The regression coefficients for the two equations are the same, but the R^2 and the standard errors are not. In order to obtain the correct standard errors, you must run the 2-Stage Least Squares procedure.

The 2-Stage Least Squares Procedure

Figure 13.8 shows the 2-Stage Least Squares results, without going through the two stages outlined above.

Figure 13.8 2-Stage Least Squares output

```
MODEL:  MOD_1.

Equation number:   1

Dependent variable.. DEMAND

Listwise Deletion of Missing Data

Multiple R          .68121
R Square            .46405
Adjusted R Square   .28540
Standard Error     2.44189

            Analysis of Variance:

            DF   Sum of Squares      Mean Square
Regression   2        30.977420        15.488710
Residuals    6        35.776864         5.962811

F =      2.59755      Signif F = .1539

Equation number:   1

Dependent variable.. DEMAND


----------------- Variables in the Equation -----------------

Variable          B        SE B       Beta        T  Sig T

PRICE       -1.265008    .616862  -2.104793   -2.051  .0862
INCOME       9.561323   4.198536   2.146960    2.277  .0630
(Constant) -40.016582  24.451868              -1.637  .1528


Correlation Matrix of Parameter Estimates

              PRICE       INCOME
PRICE     1.0000000    -.9171194
INCOME    -.9171194    1.0000000

The following new variables are being created:

  Name       Label

  FIT_1      Fit for DEMAND from 2SLS, MOD_1 Equation 1
  ERR_1      Error for DEMAND from 2SLS, MOD_1 Equation 1
```

The 2-Stage Least Squares procedure gives you the same results as two stages of OLS, with much less effort. The contrast in effort required is even more striking in larger models.

The 2-Stage Least Squares procedure is quite simple to specify. You must, however, understand the model you are estimating if you are to specify it correctly.

Appendix
Categorical Variable Coding Schemes

In many SPSS procedures, you can request automatic replacement of a categorical independent variable with a set of contrast variables, which will then be entered or removed from an equation as a block. You can specify how the set of contrast variables is to be coded, usually on the CONTRAST subcommand. This appendix explains and illustrates how different contrast types requested on CONTRAST actually work.

Deviation

Deviation from the grand mean. In matrix terms, these contrasts have the form:

```
mean    (   1/k       1/k      ...       1/k      1/k )
df(1)   ( 1-1/k      -1/k      ...      -1/k     -1/k )
df(2)   (  -1/k     1-1/k      ...      -1/k     -1/k )
  .                     .
  .                     .
df(k-1) (  -1/k      -1/k      ...     1-1/k     -1/k )
```

where k is the number of categories for the independent variable and the last category is omitted by default. For example, the deviation contrasts for an independent variable with three categories are as follows:

```
(  1/3     1/3      1/3 )
(  2/3    -1/3     -1/3 )
( -1/3     2/3     -1/3 )
```

To omit a category other than the last, specify the number of the omitted category in parentheses after the DEVIATION keyword. For example, the following subcommand obtains the deviations for the first and third categories and omits the second:

```
/CONTRAST(FACTOR)=DEVIATION(2)
```

Suppose that *factor* has three categories. The resulting contrast matrix will be

```
(   1/3       1/3       1/3 )
(   2/3      -1/3      -1/3 )
(  -1/3      -1/3       2/3 )
```

Simple

Simple contrasts. Compares each level of a factor to the last. The general matrix form is

```
mean    (   1/k       1/k      ...      1/k      1/k )
df(1)   (    1         0       ...       0       -1 )
df(2)   (    0         1       ...       0       -1 )
  .                     .
  .                     .
df(k-1) (    0         0       ...       1       -1 )
```

where k is the number of categories for the independent variable. For example, the simple contrasts for an independent variable with four categories are as follows:

```
( 1/4       1/4       1/4      1/4 )
(  1         0         0       -1 )
(  0         1         0       -1 )
(  0         0         1       -1 )
```

To use another category instead of the last as a reference category, specify in parentheses after the SIMPLE keyword the sequence number of the reference category, which is not necessarily the value associated with that category. For example, the following CONTRAST subcommand obtains a contrast matrix that omits the second category:

```
/CONTRAST(FACTOR)  =  SIMPLE(2)
```

Suppose that *factor* has four categories. The resulting contrast matrix will be

```
( 1/4       1/4       1/4      1/4 )
(  1        -1         0        0 )
(  0        -1         1        0 )
(  0        -1         0        1 )
```

Helmert

Helmert contrasts. Compares categories of an independent variable with the mean of the subsequent categories. The general matrix form is

mean	(	$1/k$	$1/k$	...	$1/k$	$1/k$)
df(1)	(	1	$-1/(k-1)$	...	$-1/(k-1)$	$-1/(k-1)$)
df(2)	(	0	1	...	$-1/(k-2)$	$-1/(k-2)$)
.			.			
.			.			
df(k-2)	(	0	0	1	$-1/2$	$-1/2$)
df(k-1)	(	0	0	...	1	-1)

where k is the number of categories of the independent variable. For example, an independent variable with four categories has a Helmert contrast matrix of the following form:

(1/4	1/4	1/4	1/4)
(1	-1/3	-1/3	-1/3)
(0	1	-1/2	-1/2)
(0	0	1	-1)

Difference

Difference or reverse Helmert contrasts. Compares categories of an independent variable with the mean of the previous categories of the variable. The general matrix form is

mean	(	$1/k$	$1/k$	$1/k$	...	$1/k$)
df(1)	(	-1	1	0	...	0)
df(2)	(	-1/2	-1/2	1	...	0)
.			.			
.			.			
df(k-1)	(	$-1/(k-1)$	$-1/(k-1)$	$-1/(k-1)$	...	1)

where k is the number of categories for the independent variable. For example, the difference contrasts for an independent variable with four categories are as follows:

(1/4	1/4	1/4	1/4)
(-1	1	0	0)
(-1/2	-1/2	1	0)
(-1/3	-1/3	-1/3	1)

Polynomial

Orthogonal polynomial contrasts. The first degree of freedom contains the linear effect across all categories; the second degree of freedom, the quadratic effect; the third degree of freedom, the cubic; and so on for the higher-order effects.

You can specify the spacing between levels of the treatment measured by the given categorical variable. Equal spacing, which is the default if you omit the metric, can be specified as consecutive integers from 1 to k, where k is the number of categories. If the variable *drug* has three categories, the subcommand

```
/CONTRAST(DRUG)=POLYNOMIAL
```

is the same as

```
/CONTRAST(DRUG)=POLYNOMIAL(1,2,3)
```

Equal spacing is not always necessary, however. For example, suppose that *drug* represents different dosages of a drug given to three groups. If the dosage administered to the second group is twice that to the first group and the dosage administered to the third group is three times that to the first group, the treatment categories are equally spaced, and an appropriate metric for this situation consists of consecutive integers:

```
/CONTRAST(DRUG)=POLYNOMIAL(1,2,3)
```

If, however, the dosage administered to the second group is four times that given the first group, and the dosage given the third group is seven times that to the first, an appropriate metric is

```
/CONTRAST(DRUG)=POLYNOMIAL(1,4,7)
```

In either case, the result of the contrast specification is that the first degree of freedom for *drug* contains the linear effect of the dosage levels and the second degree of freedom contains the quadratic effect.

Polynomial contrasts are especially useful in tests of trends and for investigating the nature of response surfaces. You can also use polynomial contrasts to perform nonlinear curve fitting, such as curvilinear regression.

Repeated

Compares adjacent levels of an independent variable. The general matrix form is

mean	($1/k$	$1/k$	$1/k$	...	$1/k$	$1/k$)
df(1)	(1	-1	0	...	0	0)
df(2)	(0	1	-1	...	0	0)
.		.				
.		.				
df(k-1)	(0	0	0	...	1	-1)

where k is the number of categories for the independent variable. For example, the repeated contrasts for an independent variable with four categories are as follows:

```
(  1/4      1/4      1/4      1/4 )
(   1       -1        0        0 )
(   0        1       -1        0 )
(   0        0        1       -1 )
```

These contrasts are useful in profile analysis and wherever difference scores are needed.

Special

A user-defined contrast. Allows entry of special contrasts in the form of square matrices with as many rows and columns as there are categories of the given independent variable. For MANOVA and LOGLINEAR, the first row entered is always the mean, or constant, effect and represents the set of weights indicating how to average other independent variables, if any, over the given variable. Generally, this contrast is a vector of ones.

The remaining rows of the matrix contain the special contrasts indicating the desired comparisons between categories of the variable. Usually, orthogonal contrasts are the most useful. Orthogonal contrasts are statistically independent and are nonredundant. Contrasts are orthogonal if:

- For each row, contrast coefficients sum to zero.

- The products of corresponding coefficients for all pairs of disjoint rows also sum to zero.

For example, suppose that *treatment* has four levels and that you want to compare the various levels of treatment with each other. An appropriate special contrast is

```
(   1        1        1        1 )     weights for mean calculation
(   3       -1       -1       -1 )     compare 1st with 2nd through 4th
(   0        2       -1       -1 )     compare 2nd with 3rd and 4th
(   0        0        1       -1 )     compare 3rd with 4th
```

which you specify by means of the following CONTRAST subcommand for MANOVA, LOGISTIC REGRESSION, and COXREG:

```
/CONTRAST(TREATMNT)=SPECIAL( 1  1  1  1
                             3 -1 -1 -1
                             0  2 -1 -1
                             0  0  1 -1 )
```

For LOGLINEAR, you need to specify:

```
/CONTRAST(TREATMNT)=BASIS SPECIAL( 1  1  1  1
                                   3 -1 -1 -1
                                   0  2 -1 -1
                                   0  0  1 -1 )
```

Each row except the means row sums to zero. Products of each pair of disjoint rows sum to zero as well:

Rows 2 and 3: $(3)(0) + (-1)(2) + (-1)(-1) + (-1)(-1) = 0$

Rows 2 and 4: $(3)(0) + (-1)(0) + (-1)(1) + (-1)(-1) = 0$

Rows 3 and 4: $(0)(0) + (2)(0) + (-1)(1) + (-1)(-1) = 0$

The special contrasts need not be orthogonal. However, they must not be linear combinations of each other. If they are, the procedure reports the linear dependency and ceases processing. Helmert, difference, and polynomial contrasts are all orthogonal contrasts.

Indicator

Indicator variable coding. Also known as dummy coding, this is not available in LOGLINEAR or MANOVA. The number of new variables coded is $k - 1$. Cases in the reference category are coded 0 for all $k - 1$ variables. A case in the ith category is coded 0 for all indicator variables except the ith, which is coded 1.

Bibliography

Agresti, A. 1990. *Categorical data analysis*. New York: John Wiley and Sons.

Aldrich, J. H., and F. D. Nelson. 1984. *Linear probability, logit, and probit models*. Beverly Hills, Calif.: Sage Publications.

Andrews, D. F., R. Gnanadesikan, and J. L. Warner. 1973. Methods for assessing multivariate normality. In: *Multivariate Analysis III*, P. R. Krishnaiah, ed. New York: Academic Press.

Atkinson, A. C. 1980. A note on the generalized information criterion for choice of a model. *Biometrika*, 67: 413–418.

Berry, W. D. 1984. *Nonrecursive causal models*. Beverly Hills, Calif.: Sage Publications.

Brown, B. W., Jr. 1980. Prediction analyses for binary data. In: *Biostatistics Casebook*, R. G. Miller, B. Efron, B. W. Brown, and L. E. Moses, eds. New York: John Wiley and Sons.

Carroll, J. D., and J. J. Chang. 1970. Analysis of individual differences in multidimensional scaling via an *n*-way generalization of "Eckart-Young" decomposition. *Psychometrika*, 35: 238–319.

Churchill, G. A., Jr. 1979. *Marketing research: Methodological foundations*. Hinsdale, Ill.: Dryden Press.

Consumer Reports. 1983. Beer. *Consumer Reports*, July, 342–348.

Draper, N. R., and H. Smith. 1981. *Applied regression analysis*. New York: John Wiley and Sons.

Finn, J. D. 1974. *A general model for multivariate analysis*. New York: Holt, Rinehart and Winston.

Finney, D. J. 1971. *Probit analysis*. Cambridge: Cambridge University Press.

Fox, J. 1984. *Linear statistical models and related methods: With applications to social research*. New York: John Wiley and Sons.

Gilbert, E. S. 1968. On discrimination using qualitative variables. *Journal of the American Statistical Association*, 63: 1399–1412.

Gill, P. E., W. M. Murray, and M. H. Wright. 1981. *Practical optimization*. London: Academic Press.

Gill, P. E., W. M. Murray, M. A. Saunders, and M. H. Wright. 1986. User's guide for NP-SOL (version 4.0): A FORTRAN package for nonlinear programming. *Technical Report SOL 86-2*. Department of Operations Research, Stanford University.

Hand, D. J. 1981. *Discrimination and classification*. New York: John Wiley and Sons.

Hanley, J. A., and B. J. McNeil. 1982. The meaning and use of the area under a receiver operating characteristic (ROC) curve. *Radiology*, 143: 29–36.

Hauck, W. W., and A. Donner. 1977. Wald's test as applied to hypotheses in logit analysis. *Journal of the American Statistical Association*, 72: 851–853.

Hosmer, D. W., and S. Lemeshow. 1989. *Applied logistic regression*. New York: John Wiley and Sons.

Jennings, L. S. 1980. Simultaneous equations estimation: Computational aspects. *Journal of Econometrics*, 12: 23–39.

Johnson, R., and D. W. Wichern. 1982. *Applied multivariate statistical analysis*. Englewood Cliffs, N.J.: Prentice-Hall.

Jonassen, C. T., and S. H. Peres. 1960. *Interrelationships of dimensions of community systems*. Columbus: Ohio State University Press.

Kaiser, H. F. 1963. Image analysis. In: *Problems in Measuring Change*, C. W. Harris, ed. Madison: University of Wisconsin Press.

_____. 1970. A second-generation Little Jiffy. *Psychometrika*, 35: 401–415.

Kelejian, H. H., and W. E. Oates. 1989. *Introduction to econometrics: Principles and applications*. 3rd ed. New York: HarperCollins.

Kirk, R. E. 1982. *Experimental design*. 2nd ed. Monterey, Calif.: Brooks/Cole.

Kleinbaum, D. 1994. *Logistic regression: A self-learning text*. New York: Springer-Verlog.

Kruskal, J. B. 1964. Nonmetric multidimensional scaling. *Psychometrika*, 29: 1–27, 115–129.

Kshirsager, A. M., and E. Arseven. 1975. A note on the equivalency of two discrimination procedures. *The American Statistician*, 29: 38–39.

Kvalseth, T. O. 1985. Cautionary note about R squared. *The American Statistician*, 39:4, 279–285.

Lawless, J. F., and K. Singhal. 1978. Efficient screening of nonnormal regression models. *Biometrics*, 34: 318–327.

Lord, F. M., and M. R. Novick. 1968. *Statistical theories of mental test scores*. Reading, Mass.: Addison-Wesley.

MacCallum, R. C. 1977. Effects of conditionality on INDSCAL and ALSCAL weights. *Psychometrika*, 42: 297–305.

McCullagh, P., and J. A. Nelder. 1989. *Generalized linear models*. 2nd ed. London: Chapman and Hall.

McGee, V. C. 1968. Multidimensional scaling of n sets of similarity measures: A nonmetric individual differences approach. *Multivariate Behavioral Research*, 3: 233–248.

Milligan, G. W. 1980. An examination of the effect of six types of error perturbation on fifteen clustering algorithms. *Psychometrika*, 45: 325–342.

Moore, D. H. 1973. Evaluation of five discrimination procedures for binary variables. *Journal of the American Statistical Association*, 68: 399.

Morrison, D. F. 1967. *Multivariate statistical methods*. New York: McGraw-Hill.

Nagelkerke, N. J. D. 1991. A note on general definition of the coefficient of determination. *Biometrika*, 78: 691–692.

Nunnally, J. 1978. *Psychometric theory*. 2nd ed. New York: McGraw-Hill.

Rao, C. R. 1973. *Linear statistical inference and its applications*. 2nd ed. New York: John Wiley and Sons.

Simonoff, J. S. 1998. Logistic regression, categorical predictors, and goodness-of-fit: It depends on who you ask. *The American Statistician,* 52: 1: 10–14.

Sneath, P. H. A., and R. R. Sokal. 1973. *Numerical taxonomy*. San Francisco: W. H. Freeman and Co.

Takane, Y., F. W. Young, and J. de Leeuw. 1977. Nonmetric individual differences multidimensional scaling: An alternating least squares method with optimal scaling features. *Psychometrika*, 42: 7–67.

Tatsuoka, M. M. 1971. *Multivariate analysis*. New York: John Wiley and Sons.

Theil, H. 1971. *Principles of econometrics*. New York: John Wiley and Sons.

Torgerson, W. S. 1952. Multidimensional scaling: I. Theory and method. *Psychometrika*, 17: 401–419.

Van Vliet, P. K. J., and J. M. Gupta. 1973. THAM v. sodium bicarbonate in idiopathic respiratory distress syndrome. *Archives of Disease in Childhood*, 48: 249–255.

Young, F. W. 1974. Scaling replicated conditional rank order data. In: *Sociological Methodology*, D. Heise, ed. American Sociological Association, 129–170.

_____. 1975. An asymmetric Euclidean model for multiprocess asymmetric data. In: *Proceedings of US–Japan Seminar on Multidimensional Scaling*.

_____. 1981. Quantitative analysis of qualitative data. *Psychometrika*, 40: 357–387.

Young, F. W., and R. M. Hamer, eds. 1987. *Multidimensional scaling: History, theory, and applications*. Hillsdale, N.J.: Lawrence Erlbaum Associates.

Young, F. W., and R. Lewyckyj. 1979. *ALSCAL–4 user's guide*. Carrboro, N.C.: Data Analysis and Theory Associates.

Simonoff, J. S. 1998. Logistic regression, categorical predictors, and goodness-of-fit: It depends on who you ask. *The American Statistician,* 52, 1: 10–14.

Index